If We Were
*Girlfriends,
This Is What I'd Tell You

BY ANDREA J. ADAMS

PANACEA PUBLISHING, AUSTIN TX
www.panaceabooks.com

If We Were Girlfriends, This Is What I'd Tell You

Copyright © 2008 by Andrea J. Adams
Published by
Panacea Publishing
Austin, TX
 www.panaceabooks.com

Cover by Jahzoe Design Company, Shawnee, Kansas
Copyediting by Susan Fitzgerald, Peachtree City, Georgia
Layout by Regroup Design, Corona, California

Library of Congress Number 2008924697
ISBN13 978-0-9743432-0-4
ISBN 9 Digits 0-9743432-0-X

This book is dedicated to Lauren,
my sweet inspiration;
I love you dearly.

Table of Contents

Foreword

"If We Were Girlfriends, This is What I'd Tell You!" is sure to become every young girl and young woman's new best friend.

Mrs. Adams addresses every key area of a girl's life and provides insightful information, wisdom and humor into the crazy, exciting, sometimes troublesome periods of a young woman's life—adolescence and young adulthood. Mrs. Adams candidly tells young women what they need to know and explains why they need to know it. Her book is a guide to enable young girls to transition into womanhood safely and securely. Her realistic examples help readers understand how the information applies to real life situations, especially their real life situations.

Every young woman in high school and college should have this book on their shelf or in their backpacks. "If We Were Girlfriends, This is What I'd Tell You!" provides young girls with a roadmap to self-awareness, relationships, finances, college and career preparation, goal setting, and most importantly being accountable and responsible for their decisions. It is an excellent book for book clubs, discussion groups, or simply a night hanging out with girlfriends.

For every mother (biological, adoptive and foster mother alike), aunt, grandmother, teacher, mentor, youth worker and youth pastor, this book is a must-read. We live in a time when too many mothers are more interested in being their daughter's friend or girlfriend instead of their mother. Adult role models, tell girls what they need to know. A desire for things and "bling" has replaced compassion for self and others. We allow our young daughters to appear in music videos as extras for fifteen seconds of fame unaware or uncaring of the emotional impact the experience has formed in their young minds that will guide their choices for years. We praise them for their ability to do the latest dances unaware of the sexual significance of those dances. They watch television and listen to music with little or no censorship from parents. Too often the parents are watching the same degrading shows with their daughters and buying sexually explicit CDs as gifts.

Although we cannot control what goes on in the world, we can control what does and does not happen in our own homes. We have allowed television and society to raise our daughters for far too long. Mrs. Adams reminds us of what we should be teaching our daughters and what our daughters should be learning about life, the world around them and themselves. "If We Were Girlfriends, This is What I'd Tell You!" will help you to help them. If we take the wisdom and knowledge contained within these pages and share them with our daughters, we may finally be able to save our daughters and change the destructive course society has paved for them.

Therefore, please do not just buy this book for your daughter, granddaughter, niece, cousin, student, or mentee. Read it yourself. As a wife, mother, mentor and educator myself, it has helped me to reflect on my own decisions made during the early seasons of my life and more importantly understand why I made the decisions I made then. It has brought understanding and closure to many of the chapters of my life and has created in me a new sense of self-awareness and empowerment. Having lost my mother at the age of sixteen, I was blessed to have other women as mentors to help me along the way. My journey still would have been a little easier and less bumpy had I had this book to help guide me.

To our mothers: If you love your daughter(s), you will read this book. To people who work with young women in high school and college: If you desire the best for them, you will read this book.

Forward

To our young high school and college women: If you love yourselves and want a roadmap to guide you through these critical years, you will read this book.

Dawn Patterson
Wife, Mother and Educator
(19+ years of working with youth)

Introduction

You are unique and special in God's eyes and each of you has something great to offer to society. You have something to offer to your community, your school, your family, your friends, church and each other as young women.

God has given each of us a talent, but it is up to us to figure out what that talent is. Your talent may be your ability to engage people or your ability to make people smile or feel good. Your talent may be singing, dancing or playing a musical instrument. You may even be talented in writing poetry, novels, or public speaking. Whatever your talent, it is important that you tap into that resource and be the best you can be at it.

I am sure many of you are probably saying you don't have a talent or don't have a clue as to what your talent is. I've heard this said many times before. To those of you who don't know what your talent is be assured that you do have one. Therefore I encourage you to explore what you are good at and what comes naturally for you. Ask others who know you well what they think you are especially good at doing. I believe that with a little investigative work on your part, you will be well on your way to finding your unique talent. To those of you who believe you don't have a talent, I challenge you to ask yourself if you believe that God would give everyone else something so special, but conveniently leave you out. Then I'll ask you to look beyond the obvious talents such as singing and dancing, and explore those things you are good at doing and feel good about doing. These traits may in fact be your talent.

In addition, I believe talents and your God-given purpose go hand in hand. Understanding and performing your God-given purpose—what it is God has put you on earth to do— may involve using your talents to do that very thing. It doesn't matter who you are, where you've come from, or what you have done in your past, God can still use you. All you have to do is make yourself available. In order to make yourself available, you must make sure you are operating at your best level both inside and out. Throughout this book, I use scriptural references for your continued reading to demonstrate, and hopefully to encourage you to see, how the Bible is a roadmap for our existence. Whether you are a Christian reading this book, a non-Christian, or aren't sure what you believe, there are certain principles that we would probably agree are important to live by that create a better living experience for us. I believe those principles can be found in the Word of God.

The purpose of this book is to provide you with a "sister girlfriend with some experience" reference. The issues addressed in this book are real to each and every one of us, and you are bound to face some of these issues at some point in your life. The issues themselves are not the challenge; the way we choose to face those issues is the challenge. Having a really clear perspective about who you are, what your purpose is, and where you are headed will help you face many of life's challenges with greater ease than if you aren't clear about where you are going.

You will be challenged by life, and you will have times in your life when you are sad or want to cry. Understanding your purpose will allow you to be down for a period; but then you can get back up because you know you have important work to do.

I wrote this book because many of the topics I discuss are issues I often wished that someone had talked openly about with me when I was a teenager. Some of the issues I raise are even applicable to girls approaching adulthood. The title I chose, "If We Were Girlfriends, This Is What I'd Tell You," was selected because I felt that often when we get together with our girlfriends we talk about things of the day, current events, music, boys, television or school, and ignore the daily issues we face. We rarely talk about our life, our dreams or how we plan to reach those dreams. We don't discuss how to save money to lead us to financial security or how to earn respect among our peers. Consequently I wrote this book to expose these necessary topics of discussion that you should be having with your peers and challenge you to have even deeper more in-depth discussions among yourselves.

I also challenge you to find your God-given purpose, live free, and learn to be comfortable with yourself.

Self Respect

Chapter 1:
Self-Respect

Webster's Dictionary defines *self-respect* as "a sense of one's own dignity or worth," it further *defines self-respect* as "a proper respect for one's self as a human being, a regard for one's own standing or position, a proper esteem or regard for the dignity of one's character."

Self-respect is synonymous with dignity, self-esteem, self-regard and pride.

Having self-respect is important because it is what defines you. Society doesn't define you; your friends don't define you; nor does the school you attend define you. The way you feel about yourself and the attitude you display daily says everything about you. Know that you define who you are. If you don't define yourself, then others will attempt to make you what they think you should be or what they want you to be.

You might be asking, "How do I define myself?" The way you define yourself is by the standards you set for yourself, the attitude you display and the moral code you live by. When people come to know you and learn who you are, the things they learn about you from their firsthand experience dealing with you, will be those character traits you display to them that give them a clear picture of who you are and what you stand for. There is a saying that says: "First impressions are lasting impressions"; and another saying that says: "You only get one chance to make a first impression." In many cases these sayings are very true. So it is always important for you to conduct yourself in a manner that truly represents who you are.

If you have aspects of your personality that you are not very proud of or are unhappy about, and would like to change those things, try to explore your options to change your behavior in those areas. If you can clearly establish that a change is necessary, then making those changes will ultimately be beneficial to you. Keep in mind, when you make a change, be sure that you are doing it because you see that it is necessary or someone you respect tells you that changing certain aspects of your personality will benefit you in some way or another. Don't just blindly change for the sake of change itself. Make sure the change will improve your life before attempting to initiate that change.

Let's look at some clear examples of when change may be necessary.

1. If you have a tendency to walk around with a frown on your face all the time, or most of the time, you may wonder why people don't appear to like you or why people refrain from approaching you. The problem may not be that they don't like you; they may think you are unapproachable and mean. While this impression may not speak the truth about who you are, your non-verbal facial expressions are sending a negative message. Think about it, a negative looking facial expression could only send a negative message. No one could ever deduce something positive from seeing a frown on your face. You are not sending a positive message with that look.

2. If you always find yourself in the middle of gossip, or if your name often comes up as the one who said something about someone, you may want to step back and take a look at your behavior. Sometimes we get caught up with talking with our friends about others, and that can prove to be unfortunate. But if this is happening frequently, more often than not, maybe you should consider changing your friends, or else change how you communicate with and about other people. You could adopt the attitude, "If you are not going to say anything nice about someone,

don't say anything at all." Remember if people hear you frequently talking about others, they will assume you are probably talking about them when they aren't around. This in turn will cause you to develop the reputation that you can't be trusted; you risk being classified as a backstabber.

3. If you tend to get angry when someone (i.e. parent, teacher, counselor, sibling) holds you accountable for your actions, then maybe you should reconsider your position on whatever they are communicating to you. Being accountable is part of becoming mature. As you get older, you need to learn how to take responsibility and be accountable for your decisions and actions. Getting angry or upset at feedback from others can often be an indication that you are immature and unable to handle constructive criticism. Subsequently you may be seen as a "cry baby." If you balk at constructive criticism, you may want to consider changing this behavior before you begin to cause people to isolate you.

While I have only given three examples, I am sure you can think of others where change may need to take place in you in order to present a better picture of yourself.

Notes

Chapter 2:
Love Yourself

Loving yourself is an essential element of self-respect. By loving yourself, I am not encouraging you to be conceited, self-absorbed, or selfish. To love yourself in a healthy way means you are not willing to allow someone to mistreat you inside or out. It means that you believe you are important and demand that others treat you with respect and common courtesy.

If you don't love yourself and respect yourself, can you expect anyone else to truly love or respect you? Let me make my point a little clearer for you. Let's say you receive a brand new pair of shoes for your birthday—a pair you've been wanting for a long time. Then after about three weeks, one of your girlfriends comes over to your house, sees these seemingly precious shoes lying on the floor with hair gel smeared on among your dirty workout clothes, and ask if she can she borrow them. You allow her to borrow them, but when she returns them to you the heel on one shoe has been broken and the other is pretty badly scratched. Your feelings are hurt, and you get very angry at your friend for being so careless with your precious shoes. While she should have taken better care of your shoes, could you really expect her to have treated them any differently than she did after she saw the condition they were in when she got them from you?

This scenario illustrates the concept of "self." If you don't take care of yourself by loving and respecting yourself, you can't expect others to treat you any better than you are willing to treat yourself. By not loving yourself, you are sending the message to others that you are not worth being loved or respected. But you *are* worthy of being loved.

Experiences can occur in your life that can take away your self-esteem or feeling of self worth. These experiences may cause you to think little of yourself and reduce your self- confidence level. This doesn't have to be your fate, remember you define who you are. Don't give anyone or anything the power to define you. If someone tells you that you won't amount to anything in life, will you give them the power to define you as "a nothing" or will you define yourself as "something" and prove them wrong?

When you were younger, you probably heard people say, "Sticks and stones will break your bones, but words will never hurt you." Well that's just not true. Words do hurt; they hurt so badly that they can even destroy a person's self-confidence. Whether you are the person saying hurtful things about someone or the person being spoken to, you should understand the impact and power those words can have. If you are being spoken of or to negatively, remind yourself that you are worthy of better, and you are beautiful despite what anyone may say about or to you. If you are the person speaking negatively about someone else, keep in mind that what you say about them can hurt them badly and may actually scar their self-image for a long time afterward.

I am acquainted with people in their 20's and 30's who are still trying to heal from things that were said to them when they were children or adolescents. Negative and hurtful comments can come from family members, classmates, and even friends. Sometimes just commenting negatively on how overweight or skinny someone is, how dark or pale their skin may be, how they have problems with acne or a certain body shape, lack of fashion in their style, or even other physical features or disabilities they have no control over just to name a few, can resonate with them for a very long time causing them to feel insecure about themselves and worthless. Don't be the type of person who builds yourself up by putting others down. You never know how your words may hurt someone. Remember, your words have power; power to hurt! So, "If you can't say anything nice about someone, don't say anything at all!"

A scripture passage that may help to remind you of how powerful your words to others may be when you find yourself in a situation where you want to speak negatively about someone, or perhaps you could share it with someone who may be speaking negatively about you is found in Ephesians. This passage says, *Do not let unwholesome talk come out of your mouths, but only what is helpful for building others up according to their needs, that it may benefit those who listen* (Eph 4:29, NIV).

People are generally good, but there are many people in the world who live their lives trying to make other people miserable. Who knows just why they do it; they just do. However you don't have to fall victim to their mean, deceitful ways. You will come up against many adversities in your life; obstacles will fall in your way and you will be tested, but those things don't define you. What defines you is how you deal with those adversities. You can deal with a challenge by crying, blaming others, becoming bitter, holding grudges, and be defeated by them. Or you can face the challenge head-on by seeing it for just what it is, a stumbling block. Create a plan of action to deal with challenges before they occur. Then when they occur, you can pick yourself up off the ground and claim victory over whatever the challenge is you are facing. Approaching the challenge from this perspective defines you as being someone who refuses to be defeated, being someone who will put up a good fight. Thank God for the adversity and praise him for using the challenge to improve you because it *will* make you stronger.

In every experience in life, whether a challenge or a victory, I urge you to learn something. Even if the lesson is "don't do it again," take that as a valuable lesson and make something good come out of it. Mistakes are typically made once (or twice), but doing the same thing over and over again and getting the same results, well, that's just not being very smart. Is it?

You should love yourself enough to want the very best for you. If you are struggling with how to love yourself, or asking the question, "What does loving myself entail," read on. In the next few chapters I discuss ways for you to get started on a journey toward loving yourself as God meant for you to love yourself.

Have you ever heard the saying, "If you don't stand for something, you will fall for anything?" Well the next chapter shows you how to get started with loving yourself by setting standards for yourself.

Notes

Chapter 3:
Set Standards for Yourself

We all have cultural standards or rules we feel we are compelled to adhere to. We have biblical standards or commandments, we must follow. We have our own personal standards we set for ourselves that tell us what we view as acceptable and not acceptable to and for us. These standards are our own! Our personal standards may be driven by our moral code, our family code, or our cultural heritage, but they are ours nonetheless.

We can't reasonably expect anyone else to adopt our personal standards except maybe when they are dealing with us directly. For example, you may not give a particular guy the time of day if he approaches you by saying, "What up, shawty," and it's ok if you don't. When he approaches you in this way, you may find such an approach to be annoying or disrespectful, and you have the right to be offended. In this circumstance the standard you are setting for yourself by not allowing him to approach you this way is that you are someone who demands more respect than he offered.

You don't need to be rude if someone does approach you with a crazy line; you can just smile politely and walk away. You don't have to respond with words; by not responding you send a very clear message. On the flip side, if you allow yourself to entertain a guy who feels it's okay to come on to you that way, you are also sending him the message that he can say other inappropriate things to you that may sound even more off the wall or vulgar. For the record, not all guys that use slang are being disrespectful. However, take into consideration that if he is really interested in you, he will want you to see a respectful well spoken gentle-man, not one who tries to impress with slang and improper grammar. There's nothing wrong with wanting to be cool, but being *cool* has never equated to act-ing like a *fool*.

The same sort of personal standard can be applied to the dress code you will accept for yourself as well as the young men you hangout with. While it may look cool or be in fashion for guys to walk around with their pants hanging off their behinds, to have their hats and shirts looking any kind of way, or for girls to wear clothing that is too small or exposes cleavage, it's not cute nor is it showing anyone that you have respect for yourself when you engage or participate in such displays.

The way you dress speaks volumes about you. People make determinations about you based on the way you dress. Of course, this is a form of judging, but if a person "judged" you the way you wanted them to judge you (meaning they get it right) based on how you dress, then you won't have a problem with what they say if you dress conservatively. When you dress appropriately, you won't feel that you are being judged wrongly. Take that same attitude with the understand-ing that people will judge you regardless and make sure that your dress code is communicating the right thing about you. Dress in a way that says you respect yourself and expect others to respect you as well.

Parents and the average adult certainly understand the importance of young people attempting to create their own identities and express themselves through being creative. However some forms of expression just aren't necessary. Clothing may not be the arena in which you wish to express yourself if it results in express-ing yourself in a way you do not intend. If you are opposed to a particular type of attire, then this would be a standard you'd set for yourself and others you choose to deal with.

Setting standards you will use to lead you through life is not placing yourself in a seat to judge. It simply helps you create some guidelines for what is and is not acceptable in your life. If you start to feel that you are judging people by setting too high of a personal standard, use this little test below to help keep you on the right track and to assure yourself that you aren't judging the people around you.

Testing the standard:

1. Is my standard fair (would most people see this as ok)?

2. Am I judging something about someone that they cannot change?

3. Is my standard realistic? Could one really be held to this standard without issue?

4. Am I flexible with this standard, and if so, to what extent?

If you find your standard to be fair, and you are basing your standard on behaviors alone, and your standards appear to be realistic, then you probably are not guilty of judging another. Just make sure you always keep an open mind and remain flexible to the extent that you feel comfortable.

Notes

Chapter 4:
Believe in Yourself

Another aspect of loving yourself is believing in yourself. *I can do all things through Christ who strengthens me* (Phil 3:14, NIV).

Whatever you set your mind to do, believe that you can/will do it. Believing in yourself is the key to success because if *you* believe you can do something, you are more likely to strive hard to accomplish your goal. Allow your dreams to become your reality. Once your dream is conceived, it must be birthed and then nurtured.

Never allow anyone to cause you to feel you are incapable, inadequate, incompetent or unable to do something you set out to do. People will try to discourage you from realizing your dreams, but *try* to derail you is all they should be able to do. When you feel confident in yourself, and you have the belief that you can do anything, you can.

Never allow anyone to tell you that you can't achieve your goals, realize your dreams, or be something you desire. God made you and only he knows your full potential. No one but God can determine what the outcome will be for you. *Let us fix our eyes on Jesus, the author and finisher of our faith, who for the joy set before him endured the cross, scorning its shame, and sat down at the right hand of the throne of God* (Heb 12:2, NIV).

In reality, everything you try your hand at may not turn into something big. But the fact that you believe in yourself enough to even try shows your drive and determination towards getting the things you want in life.

Very few people are good at everything they do; some people are just bold enough and believe in themselves enough to go for what they want. You don't have to be a superstar in everything, or anything for that matter, but having the belief that you are just as capable as the next person is all you need to succeed in your dreams.

If you strive for something and come up short, don't give up. Regroup, find your niche, and go at it again. Failure is often part of success. You have to try until you get it right, or at least until you realize that the particular activity, profession, or relationship is not for you. Even when you don't succeed, you can still be successful in that: 1) you believed in yourself enough to try that particular thing; and 2) you learned a lesson (even if the lesson is that you don't need to spend anymore time doing that particular thing because it's not for you). Believe in yourself and achieve great things in life because you can!

Notes

Chapter 5:
Can Anyone Get You to Do Something You Don't Want to Do?

Can anyone get you to do something you don't want to do? Think about that question for a few minutes. Your body is God's temple. If your body is God's temple, and he dwells in that temple, how long do you think he will stay there if you're allowing his temple to be abused? *Do you not know that your body is a temple of the Holy Spirit, who is in you, whom you have received from God? You are not your own; you were bought with a price. Therefore honor God with your body* (Cor 6:19-20, NIV).

You can abuse or allow your body to be abused in many ways. Anything from drinking alcohol excessively (or underage drinking), or smoking harmful substances like marijuana, crack, or drugs to allowing someone to physically or sexually abuse you are all ways that your body can be abused.

If you have been a victim of sexual or physical abuse in which you were taken advantage of because you were helpless and couldn't protect yourself, then you are not to blame for what happened to you. If you have not told anyone about this, you should reconsider your decision not to tell, and tell someone. Talking to someone who has experience working with victims of abuse can be the beginning of a lifetime of healing for you. You must come to understand that what happened to you is not your fault. Regardless of what anyone has told you, you did and do not deserve to be abused in any way. Perhaps someone who didn't feel loved, appreciated or cared for is unable to deal with those feelings, and in turn took their pain out on you. They need to get help for what they experienced as a victim, but they haven't, and consequently, they victimized someone else, maybe you.

If you have been a victim of sexual, physical or emotional abuse, you don't have to remain a "victim." Getting the help you need to deal with what has happened to you by talking to a trusted adult is the first step to healing. The second step to healing is changing your mindset about being a victim. The day you decide to stop being a victim is also the day you become a survivor. You no longer allow what has happened to you define who you are or what you will become. You no longer live each day afraid to go on with your life. You continue to pursue your dreams and face each day with confidence. The healing process begins the moment you transform from victim to survivor. By redefining yourself as a survivor, you serve notice to your perpetrator(s) that you are victorious and will not be held back because of what they have done.

Your life does not end when something bad happens. You may feel as though your world is over; you may feel lonely and/or alone in this world; or you may feel like you want to hurt yourself, even to the point of wanting to take your own life. The pain of dealing with abuse can stir up many negative emotions. Please be assured that someone is always available to help you. You do not have to go through this ordeal alone. The person who took advantage of you is not worth your unhappiness or your desires to hurt yourself. Please speak to someone you trust about your abuse. You may be the one person who has enough courage to stop this person from abusing or hurting someone else.

Notes

Chapter 6:
Abusing Your Temple
or Allowing Someone Else to Abuse It.

Being helpless to abuse is obviously not the same as allowing someone to abuse you. You may be thinking abuse is abuse, isn't it all the same? Not exactly! You may even be thinking, "Why on earth, would someone allow themselves to be abused?" Most people who "allow" themselves to be abused don't see it as abuse, at least not at first. They may not ever see it as abuse until someone else points it out to them. It may not be until someone brings it to their attention that they come to see a particular behavior as abuse.

If you are under the age of 21, and you are using alcohol, that is irresponsible of you as well as illegal. Making a decision to use illicit drugs at any age, well that too, is irresponsible and illegal. Sure, you may have friends or know people who use alcohol or drugs, but this doesn't mean you have to follow their lead and participate too. If someone tries to get you to do anything you know isn't in your best interest, be bold in your commitment to keep your temple clean. Even if you are using alcohol or drugs now or have in the past, you don't have to continue abusing your temple in this way.

Chapter 9 deals in depth on relationships, but right now I want to highlight some specifics about relationships and abuse. If you are in a relationship in which you are being physically, verbally, emotionally, or sexually abused, Please get out now! It doesn't matter how long you have been in this relationship, you can still get out. Anyone who is willing to hurt you, your body or break you down emotionally is not worth having in your life. If that person is a parent or "loved one," get help immediately from a trusted adult.

Someone who says they love you, but calls you names, tells you lies, hits you, or encourages you to use drugs or alcohol, does not have your best interest at heart. If you make a commitment to yourself and God that you will keep your body clean and pure, but allow someone to talk you into doing something that is contrary to that commitment, then you have failed yourself and God. No one or no relationship should be worth that sacrifice. Furthermore, any decisions made about your body should be made by you and you alone. No one should be able to make you do something that you don't want to do. If you are allowing people to think for you and make decisions for you, then you are giving someone power and authority over you that they have no right to possess. You can't get angry with the outcome of a situation if you didn't stand up and take control over your body.

In addition, are you aware that you are abusing your temple by participating in premarital sex? You are additionally abusing your temple if you are having multiple sex partners. Abusing your temple by ingesting harmful substances is yet another way you can abuse your temple.

Many negatives come out of hurting God's temple. Not only are you hurting your physical body when you abuse your temple, but you are also hurting your psychological self, the part of your self that deals with emotions and feelings. You cannot get back years of repeated poor choices. While you may feel good about what you are doing at a particular moment, whether it be a sexual high or drug induced high, those pleasant feelings don't last. They are only temporary feelings. The feelings that tend to linger are feelings of shame and guilt for what you have done. While God is forgiving (1 John 1:9), we often hang on to the shame of our past. I encourage you to make wise, smart and safe choices so that you don't have to experience the shame and/or guilt later on down the line.

I often hear adults talk about how if they had a chance to do certain things over again, they would do them differently. When I hear these comments, the people who make them may not always be talking about something they are ashamed of or feel guilty about, but sometimes they are. The tragic aspect of these stories or experiences is when we come to a fork in the road and even though the two paths are very clear cut, we choose to take the path that leads to destruction. Why is this tragic? It is tragic because you too will be sitting somewhere in the future saying, "If I had the chance to do it all over again, I would do things differently." This is not to say that we won't make mistakes in our lives. Mistakes often help us to grow. However poor choices can lead to rough times, and getting back on track may not always be easy. Just one poor life choice may cause you to waste a lot of time regretting or feeling ashamed about your past.

Here's an example of what I am talking about. Let's say a 15-year-old girl has several boyfriends throughout her sophomore year of high school. While dating these boys, she makes a choice to have sex with each of them. One of these boys encourages her to get high with him one day before having sex. That unlucky night while under the influence she fails to use protection and gets pregnant. She doesn't know that the blunt she smoked was laced with crack. Over time she allows this boyfriend to continue giving her laced blunts and has sex with her. Then one fateful day, she finds out that she is pregnant. By this time, she is hooked on drugs and learns that in addition to her addiction, she has an STD. Guess what? She doesn't know who the STD came from (because she has had many sexual partners) and fears her baby may have been exposed to drugs while in the womb. She later delivers her baby only to learn that her baby has some minor birth defects caused by her drug use. After the baby is born, her boyfriend wants nothing else to do with her or the baby. She meets new guys all the time, but when they find out she has a baby, they quickly become uninterested. The one good thing about this experience is she no longer uses drugs. However she has to live every day looking at her child she didn't plan who has special needs. Well into her late teenage years she sits around regretting what she did and the poor choices she made. She often thinks about the many times she had the opportunity to say "No" to drugs and "No" to sex, but chose not to.

While this scenario is only an example, it does really happen. The point I hope to make here is: Learn to take time to think before you act. More often than not, if you think about what could happen down the line as a result of your choice today, you might actually make a better choice. Keep in mind, the choices you make today will determine your tomorrow.

My challenge to you is to always think long and hard about the decisions you make and ask yourself, "If I do this one thing does it have the *potential* to be life altering in a good way or a bad way?" Notice the operative word here is potential. Don't allow anyone to encourage you to do anything without giving it some thought first. When it comes to your temple, you are the one, and only one, that has the right to say "Yes" or "No" because you will have to live with the long-term results of your decisions.

Notes

Chapter 7:
Beauty,
Is It Really Only Skin Deep?

Your beauty should not come from outward adornment, such as braided hair and the wearing of gold jewelry and fine clothes. Instead, it should be that of your inner self, the unfading beauty of a gentle and quiet spirit which is of a great worth in God's sight (I Pet 3:3-4, NIV).

Accepting yourself and loving yourself in every way is important. Someone out there will always be prettier than you. We can all find things about ourselves that we don't like or wish we could change. We can pay a lot of money to enhance our breasts, noses, calves, lips—the list could go on. Just remember, changing ourselves from the outside results only in an outside change.

Take a moment to think about change. While we may present ourselves to the world as a glamorous diva, it's what's on the inside that truly matters. At the end of the day, beauty goes deeper than our skin's surface. You may be saying, "But if that's true, then why do all the pretty girls get the guys?" They don't! Males are visual creatures and their eyes are drawn to things that are appealing to their eyes. Physical beauty may be what *gets* the guy, but what's on the inside is what *keeps* the guy. If you happen to be beautiful inside and out, then you are truly a sight to behold. All you need to do is sit back and wait for your prince.

What do I mean by being beautiful inside and out? If you have a pretty face but a nasty or bad attitude, then you are only beautiful on the outside, and are missing some very much needed beauty on the inside. If you have a pretty face and are kind to people and have a loving spirit, then people will see you as being beautiful inside and out. If you are not very attractive, but you have a loving spirit and people are drawn to you because of your personality, then people will consider you to be a beautiful person. I think it is important to understand these truths about beauty because outer beauty can and will ultimately fade away. Whereas inner beauty just gets more and more beautiful with time.

At the tender age of fifteen years old, you may not be able to even fathom what you might look like at thirty, let alone at fifty. But for argument's sake, try to go here with me for a minute. Think of older pictures of your mother or grandmother you may have seen of her when she was your age or in her early twenties, then think of how she looks now. She may still be very attractive, but as time has passed you may notice that her skin may not be as tight as it used to be giving way to fine lines or wrinkles. Her body may not be holding its once coveted curves. Those may have started to disappear. But she is still dear to her loved ones and just as loved by them as ever.

Beauty does eventually fade, whether you can imagine it or not. But the question is can your inner beauty sustain you?

Having a bad attitude makes a person ugly even if they look pretty. I think there are a lot of personality traits that create ugliness in someone who appears to be pretty on the outside. For example, a lying tongue, a deceitful heart, a jealous heart, excessive cursing, a nasty attitude or even a mean spirit are all character deficits that can destroy a pretty image over time.

The saying, "You shouldn't judge a book by its cover," holds true in many instances. What is on the outside cover may not always line up with what is on the inside. Be careful to make sure your inside mirrors your outside.

Eventually anyone who does not have a beautiful spirit, and instead hides behind their looks will be found out. Character traits that are deeply rooted in an individual's personality can not be covered up by good looks for very long. If negative traits are part of an individual, those negative traits will inevitably push through the veneer of beauty and be front and center for everyone to see.

So when you contemplate asking, "Why is it that the pretty girls get all the guys," take heart, in the real world pretty girls don't get all the guys. These so-called *pretty girls* don't get the guy and keep him because their true self is revealed at some point, proving to not be worth the effort of the guy they think they have snagged. Just keep in mind you must have more going for you than a pretty face and/or a *hot* body to sustain a long-term, loving relationship. Having a kind and loving heart will always take you much further than a pretty face or a cute figure.

Notes

Chapter 8:
Your Heritage
Where Do You Come From?
What Legacy Do You Want to Leave?

So you are no longer a slave, but a son, and since you are a son, God has made you also an heir (Gal 4:7, NIV). According to this verse, you originate from God, which makes you a joint heir with Jesus Christ. Being a joint heir with Jesus Christ is significant because that means everything God gives to Jesus Christ is also available to you.

A large part of establishing self-respect is having an understanding of your heritage. That is, understanding where you come from, your lineage, and more importantly, realizing that you are a child of God, and as a result you have purpose in this world.

Knowing your family's heritage is equally important because your family heritage gives you a basis from which you can build on. Understanding your family's struggles, triumphs, high points and low points can give you a clear picture of where your strengths come from and what your greatest challenges in life may be.

It's not often that when we're young, we desire to take a seat next to an older person in the family to just spend time and talk with them, but you should. The older members of the family are the ones who hold all the information about the family's history. They have been here longer and can tell you more than anyone else about your heritage. An older relative's perspective may be enlightening about certain aspects of your personality.

If you come from a long line of farmers, doctors, lawyers, teachers, home-makers, preachers or whatever, that is information you may need to know. Having a clear understanding of your family's values, beliefs and customs gives you a sense of self. These aspects of your family are a part of who you are.

You may be asking, "What if I come from a long line of drug dealers, pimps, prostitutes, adulterers, and felons?" Remember I mentioned earlier how understanding your family can also give you insight into what your greatest challenges may be in life. Not all family background is pretty; but is helpful to your personal development nevertheless. If you happen to come from a family infamous for things that don't particularly make you proud, this could be challenging for you in that you may have to work harder to prove that you are not a product of your heritage and destined to repeat the mistakes of your ancestors. You may have to work hard to pull yourself out of that negative mentality and perception of yourself. Remember, God has a plan for *your* life, and that plan does not include anything that would bring shame to God or you.

While your family's heritage doesn't necessarily define you as an individual, where you come from has a huge impact on you and your life. You must make your own path and decide for yourself the direction you will take. Having a clear picture about your family is important in helping you get to where you want to go. Here's how, if your family heritage is shameful and you know how it got to be that way, then you can resolve to make choices to do things differently. You can resolve and initiate a plan to not follow those same paths that created the reputation for your family. If your family heritage makes you proud, then you can make choices in your own life that will preserve your family's heritage and continue to bring pride to your family.

Finally, as you begin to establish your own place in society, the question you should ask yourself is, "What will my legacy be?" When you move from one place to another, city to city, state to state, country to country, or even job to job, what do you want people to say about you after you leave? How do you want people to remember you? What memories will you leave along the way? Will people say positive things about you, or will they remember you in a negative way?

We are all products of our environments, but you are ultimately responsible for creating your own image and becoming the best you can be. Being your best is your responsibility and yours alone. You must take time to nurture your dreams because you can't expect anyone else to nurture them for you. You must take time to encourage yourself and affirm daily that you are beautiful inside and out regardless of what images are displayed on magazine covers. Challenge yourself to strive higher than you did yesterday because seeing the results of what you have worked so hard to accomplish builds your confidence and your self esteem.

As I bring this section on self respect to a close, I want to stress the importance of why loving yourself is the key to being emotionally healthy. Loving and respecting yourself is by and large the foundation for how you treat others and how others treat you. Remember if you don't love and respect yourself, how can you expect others to treat you with love and respect? On the other hand, if you don't love and respect yourself, it is unlikely you will be able to truly love and respect anyone else. Love and respect for others as well as love and respect for yourself all starts within you.

Notes

Relationships

Chapter 9:
Healthy
Relationships

This chapter is about a particularly sensitive subject to me because my hearts breaks each time I work with a young woman who has had her heart broken by someone. Relationships come in various forms. A relationship can be between a mother and her daughter, a mother and her son, a sister and her brother, a father and his son, a father and his daughter, a teacher and a student, a grandmother and her granddaughter, a boyfriend and a girlfriend, two friends, etc. There are countless ways to be engaged in a relationship. Relationships form for many reasons and can end for many reasons. When some relationships end, it can be difficult for one or all parties involved to disengage and accept that the relationship is over or at least different from what it was previously. Occasionally a relationship ends, and it's a good thing for all parties involved whether the ending is a difficult one or not.

Relationships are a necessary aspect for our lives. When our relationships are healthy ones, they add great value to our lives (i.e., they bring us laughter, security, peace, joy). When our relationships are unhealthy, they add very little value to our lives and may even create stress, anxiety, fear, frustrations, sadness, and anger in us. Negative feelings toward another individual may eventually turn into resentment and bitterness that sometimes remain with us for a very long time. Think about some of the relationships you are in, or have been engaged in previously, and determine if they are healthy or unhealthy. "How can I tell if a particular relationship is healthy or not," you may ask.

Let's first explore some important elements of any relationship—trust, honesty, loyalty, respect, commitment, forgiveness and effective communication (and whatever else you deem to be important to you). These elements must be present in any relationship for it to be even modestly successful. If these things are not present in a particular relationship, then that relationship may have difficulty thriving.

Trust is a significant factor in relationships. Trust is the foundation for any relationship and must exist if the relationship is to survive and thrive. If trust is suppose to be the foundation and trust does not exist, then you have nothing on which to build the rest of the relationship. So if you try to continue a relationship without trust, you only get suspicion, chaos, anxiety and frustration. These elements do not add value to your life.

Let's look at a relationship from the standpoint of building a house. When you build a house, the first thing you have to do is lay the foundation; foundations are typically laid by using a concrete base. Why, because concrete is hard and not easily destroyed. Concrete can handle the weight of the other parts of the house that will be placed on top of it to complete the structure. Once the foundation in a house is laid, it dries and becomes solid. If you try to build a house and don't lay a concrete foundation, nothing else you build onto the house will matter because the house won't have anything on the bottom to hold it, so it will fall apart. If you try to build a house on a weak foundation or one that is not allowed to dry completely, then the walls of the house will start to crack. This too could end in disaster because anything else you try to add to the house would not stand due to the lack of support of a firm foundation.

Similar to the construction of a house with its concrete foundation, a relationship needs to have trust as the foundation or it will not be successful. If the trust you have for an individual is weak or shaky, it's only a matter of time before you'll begin to see other areas of the relationship suffer.

If someone does something that hurts you or causes you to lose your trust in them, it may take a while before you can begin to trust them again. In some instances, trusting them again may not be possible. While trust is the foundation for relationships and would normally denote strength in the relationship, once trust is broken the relationship becomes fragile. Once betrayed, trust is hard to reestablish. So whether it's you or someone you care about, remember once trust is broken, it's hard to get back. Think long and hard about your actions and words before you do something that will break someone's trust in you.

This is true in any relationship you have. Trust can be broken when you do something your parents specifically tell you not to do or go some place they tell you not to go. You may not think it is a big deal because no one will get hurt or nothing bad will happen, but your disobedience is a bigger deal than that. If your parents give you a certain degree of freedom to make good choices based on the criteria they set forth and you do the complete opposite, you will break the trust they have in you to do what you all agreed you will do. This behavior begins to set a pattern with your parents that can leave them unwilling to give you freedom to do certain things because you have broken their trust. Depending on what you may do to break their trust, it may be a hard road getting back to having them trust you the same way again. This circumstance is no different than having your parent or parents make promises or commitments to you over and over again but not follow through on those promises. If you come to a place where you don't trust what they say, they should not be surprised when you lose trust in them. Trust in a relationship goes both ways, even in a parent /child relationship.

However, do not use lack of trust for your parents as an excuse to be disrespectful. Even if your parents have disappointed you in some way or another time after time, you are still required to respect them. Respect may be hard to display at times since trust is a significant part of a relationship, but the word of God tells us that we must forever honor our parents. ***Honor your father and your mother, so that you may live long in the land your God is giving you*** (Exod 20:12 NIV).

Honesty is another element that should exist in a relationship. I could assume that the importance of honesty in a relationship goes without saying, but I will explain anyway. Being honest is one way to build trust; lying is one way to tear it down. Go figure, not that difficult to understand is it? For some it may not be as cut and dry as I have insinuated; especially if they are use to lying and being dishonest and getting away with it. What is often amusing is when the person telling the lies or being dishonest thinks they are getting away with it and that nobody has a clue. That may be true in some instances, but most of the time people know the liar is lying and choose not to confront them because they believe that a confrontation will result in more lies or make the situation worse. By not arguing or confronting that individual, the victim of a liar is left feeling taken advantage of, while the liar basks in having somehow gotten something over on his victim. The liar assumes that no one is the wiser to his deceit, but his victim may be secretly laughing to himself/herself thinking how sad it must be to have a lying heart and to actually think you're getting away with it. What this individual is not taking into consideration is the fact they may be tearing down the trust others may have had in them.

The Bible talks about a lying tongue throughout. I don't know of anyone who wants to have the reputation of being a liar. Most normal people do not aspire to have that reputation, but when they make lying and dishonesty a part of their daily lives and conversation, it becomes who they are and how they are perceived. One passage of scripture in particular tells us how we should deal with a lying tongue. *Therefore each of you must put off falsehood and speak truthfully to his neighbor, for we are all members of one body* (Eph 4:25, NIV).

People lie for many reasons and justify their dishonesty. Anyone can justify why they do anything they do, and I don't want to judge harshly on that. What I will say, however, is that in the case of relationships, no matter how the relationship is defined, lying to get something over on someone, manipulating them, assassinating someone's character, hurting them or controlling them is wrong; it qualifies as both unhealthy and unGodly behavior.

Some people talk about little white lies and ask, "Is it wrong to tell a 'little white lie?'" A lie is a lie regardless of the color, right? The reality is, we all have told lies whether big or small, but you must determine for yourself if what you are doing or what someone is doing to you in the way of lying or being dishonest is harmful to you and/or the success of your relationship. Keep in mind, lies don't heal relationships; they kill relationships; and once you tell a lie you will have to tell another lie to cover up the lie you already told, and the cycle continues around that lie.

So I advise you to take the high road in the things you do—be honest and truthful. Consequently your reputation will be one that you can be proud of. People will have a greater respect for you, a desire to be in your company and a willingness to deal with you rather than not. You will also have a greater respect for yourself when you are honest. It may feel hard at times to tell the truth and be honest. However, honesty is always best, if for no other reason then that you'll go to sleep each night with a clear conscious and a clean heart.

Loyalty is about being there for someone in the good and bad times. It's about going the distance with them when they need you. Loyalty means not stabbing someone in the back to get their boyfriend or their job. It means not turning your back on a friend when you can't have your way. Loyalty means not allowing someone else to talk about a friend in a negative way under any circumstance.

Loyalty is important in all relationships because you need to know that the person you are calling "friend" is someone you can count on to be there for you. However, I must say, being loyal is important to a degree. Let me explain. You don't have to be loyal to your friend, family, or boyfriend, if being loyal causes you to be harmed physically, emotionally, psychologically or sexually in any way. You don't have to prove you are loyal by taking the blame for something someone else has done; especially if the deed is a criminal one. Actually, that would not be loyalty; that would be stupidity. Loyalty is about support, encouragement, protection and edification. You can show your loyalty for someone by standing up for them when you know they've done nothing wrong, but everyone is against them. Jesus' disciples were, for the most part, loyal to him (with the exception of Peter and Judas). They followed him, supported his mission, defended him against those who talked against him and spread his gospel. Talk about being a loyal friend. Jesus' disciples were loyal friends. Having someone in your corner, someone like a disciple is worthwhile. But to the contrary, having someone who claims to be "down" with you, yet causes you confusion, and brings you sadness and frustration is not a friend and does not fall into the healthy relationship category.

Respect is another important element necessary in a relationship. Respect is important because it essentially communicates to another person how you feel about them. If you are disrespectful to someone, then you are communicating to them that you don't think very highly of them and there is very little you wouldn't do to hurt them. If you are respectful to others and they are respectful to you, you are communicating that you have regard for them and their feelings and you are going to do whatever necessary to preserve the relationship.

When someone respects you, they don't hurt you with their lies. They don't hurt you with their hands. They don't hurt you with their tongue by calling you names or saying mean things to you. And they don't hurt you by neglecting you.

As I mentioned in the previous section, you must respect yourself if you are going to expect others to treat you with respect. If you respect yourself, it will be very hard for you to allow someone to disrespect you. Be cautious, people who are good at hurting others aren't always blatant about their disrespect. Oftentimes they will complain that you are overreacting or making a big deal out of something they did and you should calm down about it; but if you feel you have been disrespected by what they have done, then that's all that matters. No one can tell you how you feel or how to feel. It's good to confront people by letting them know when you feel disrespected and ask them to please not do that again. If you find that things like this happen often with a particular person, and you have to bring it to their attention frequently without changes in the relationship, then you may want to categorize this as an unhealthy person to have a relationship with. The chances of that person changing during the course of your relationship/friendship after you have repeatedly brought the problem to their attention, is pretty slim. You may need to cut your losses and move on.

Cutting your losses is sometimes hard to do for various reasons. While it may be necessary throughout your life to end relationships, it may not be the easiest thing to do. In some cases it may be very hard to end a relationship, especially one with a family member. Instead of trying to end it in this case, you may need to distance yourself from that individual but not sever the relationship with a hope that change may occur at some point.

Relationship dynamics can be complicated and stressful. The most important thing to take away from this information is to try to have a clear picture of who you are dealing with and making sure you are getting the respect you deserve.

Let us not forget about forgiveness. God tells us that we are to forgive no matter what the situation and continue forgiving a person even when they wrong us repeatedly. He says to do this because he forgives us over and over when we do wrong and sin against him. Forgiving challenges us to our core sometimes, especially depending on what we are forgiving someone for. It may be easy to forgive a friend who forgets to pick you up from work on the coldest day of the year even though you ended up getting a ride from a coworker, and you weren't left in the cold for very long. However, it might be a lot more difficult to forgive that same friend who gets tickets to the hottest concert (your favorite group) in town and decides to take her boyfriend who doesn't even like the group at all. Just like in a court of law, there are different degrees to offenses, and certainly there are times when we may find it easier to forgive and other times it may be harder. Regardless the degree of the offense, we must forgive.

Learning to forgive is important because holding onto hurt and pain caused by someone who has wronged you only eats away at you. If you are harboring negative feelings towards someone who has done something to you in the past or recently, forgive them for your sake; let it go and move on. Even if your offender is a family member, close or distant, forgive them and move on. There is nothing worse than being angry with someone for years when they don't even know you feel anger or hurt toward them. When you hold onto this anger you are allowing this person to control your feelings without them even knowing they have this kind of power over you. A person who has offended you may remember doing so, but may not have any idea that you are still mad about it six months or even 2 years later.

In many cases it's not feasible to actually go to that person and verbally forgive them. For whatever reason face to face contact may not be possible, and that's okay. Forgiveness begins in your heart where you make a decision to pardon that person's behavior. After you make the decision to forgive, then you act on that decision from your heart by no longer holding anger or bitterness against them. Test yourself when that person's name comes up or you happen to come face to face with them to determine how far along you are in your forgiveness toward them. When this interaction takes place, if you are able to sincerely be cordial or friendly, speak without an angry tone or rolling your eyes, or walk away without any past negative emotions welling up inside you, then you know that you have truly forgiven them.

Forgiving may be challenging at times, but keep this in mind, most people who have done something to hurt someone else don't realize that the one they hurt feels so strongly about them, and probably wouldn't care if they did know. So how does it benefit you to hold a grudge, robbing yourself of peace and happiness over something someone did that hurt you, but they don't know or care that it actually impacted you the way it did? It doesn't benefit you at all. Forgiveness brings about a certain degree of peace in your life. Besides, do you really want wrinkles on your forehead and around your mouth caused by all that frowning because you're angry all the time and not as a result of getting older? I have heard, but haven't confirmed it through research, that over time certain physical problems can come about due to holding anger inside and harboring negative feelings towards people for long periods of time. I actually believe this is true, and I don't want to personally prove the theory, so I'd rather forgive.

Healthy relationships are not one-sided. This means one person doesn't do all the giving and the other person doesn't do all the taking in the relationship. There may be times when it feels like you are giving, giving, giving and not getting anything in return. This is reality, but it should balance itself out sooner rather than later. If it doesn't, then you should reconsider your relationship with anyone you are involved with where you feel so taken advantage of.

Healthy relationships aren't always about love or being in love. While some male/female relationships take on those emotions, those emotions don't have to exist in order for the relationship to be healthy; respect must exist. If someone respects you, they will have your best interest at heart and will not hurt you. Healthy relationships are fulfilling and mutual; they should enhance your life, not make it more stressful.

Notes

Chapter 10:
Communication and Relationships

Communication plays an important role in relationships. Effective communication in any relationship is a must. Notice I said effective communication. We communicate all the time, but not always effectively.

What is communication? Webster's *dictionary defines* communication as "a process by which meanings are exchanged between individuals through a common system of symbols. It is transferring or exchanging information." There are two forms of communication. Verbal communication is when you are using language to transfer or exchange information, speaking rather than writing. Non-verbal communication is the use of gestures, symbols, sounds and body language rather than spoken words to transfer or exchange information.

Non-verbal communication can take on both positive and negative forms. Some positive examples of non-verbal communication are smiling, hugging, nodding, lifting hands (in praise), and clapping. Some negative examples of non-verbal communication are rolling your eyes, folding your arms, rolling your neck, twisting your lips, turning your shoulder, turning your back to someone, stomping your feet, and walking away.

Tone is another important aspect of communication. Your tone has a major impact on how your message is received. *Tone* is defined as "an accent or inflection expressive of a mood or emotion." For example, if you holler or yell a command, it will be received very differently from the command spoken in a calm voice.

Carefully choosing the words you use to communicate with is important. While many words have the same meaning, certain words can be taken offensively or cause someone to become defensive. For example, using the words *always* or *never* to describe someone's actions can make them uncomfortable and cause them to become defensive.

If you hear someone say, "You never give me any money to go shopping," you know they are exaggerating. First of all, if you say this you are not communicating the truth because I'm sure at some point in time you've been given money to go shopping. Secondly, when using the word *never*, you would not be acknowledging the times that you have been given money to go shopping or do anything else. Such exaggerated statements communicates that you are ungrateful or unappreciative of what the person you are complaining to *has* done for you.

So, in order to send the person the real message you want them to hear, you must choose your words more carefully. You might be asking, does this mean I must walk on eggshells in order to make sure I am communicating exactly what I want people to hear? Does walking on eggshells mean the same as choosing my words carefully?

No! *Walking on eggshells* means you are afraid to communicate your feelings or thoughts for fear of how another person will respond to you. Walking on eggshells is a practice that keeps you from being who you are and expressing yourself. Over time this feeling will cause you to become timid and shy about speaking out and expressing yourself.

Choosing your words carefully, on the other hand, is simply making sure that what you want to say is exactly what you are saying. To choose your words carefully means you are not using words that can be taken offensively or be upsetting to others.

Remember, it is important for you to be expressive and open with your feelings in a way that is helpful, not hurtful and loving, not hateful. Effective communication is a powerful skill to master as a young women; it displays self-confidence and will yield much respect from your peers and others around you!

Everything I have said thus far about relationships is applicable to relationships of all types (i.e. mother/daughter, sisters, sister/brother, friends, cousins, etc.), but what I want to address next deals specifically with male/female relationships.

Keeping in mind all the things I noted earlier as necessary elements in a relationship, specifically trust, honesty, loyalty, and respect, you should choose your boyfriend wisely. Marriage seems so far off right now that you probably don't think much about it. But when you decide to date a guy, make that decision as if you are choosing someone you could and would spend the rest of your life with. You are probably asking, "Why should I do that if I am a teenager or in my early twenties and only want to have a good time? If you only want to have a good time, then hang out with friends, males and females, and don't allow yourself to become romantically involved. Not being romantically involved means no kissing too! I advise you to choose a boyfriend as if you are choosing a spouse because once you begin to set certain criteria that you will use to select a mate, you will quickly learn that every guy does not possess the characteristics of someone you'd want to be with long-term. If a particular guy doesn't exhibit the characteristics of someone who is following Christ to begin with, steer clear. If he is not Godly, then he will not be able to give you the respect you deserve. He may be a nice guy and have a beautiful smile, but down the line those things will not be enough to sustain your relationship.

Even at your age, a young man should know how to pray, read and follow the scriptures in the Bible, as the bible is our roadmap for life. He should understand that making a decision to have Christ in his life is the most important decision he could ever make. This young man should be more interested in helping you understand the word of God than how tight your jeans are or if you want to have sex or not. Finding someone who is God-fearing and committed to doing God's will is a blessing to have in your life. It's not enough for an individual to accept Christ into his/her life, living a life that is pleasing to God is also required.

Throughout your life you will probably encounter many guys you find attractive and may become interested in dating. I would encourage you to make a list of all the characteristics you want your future mate to possess. Keep that list handy, and when you meet someone you find interesting, hold him up to that list to see how closely he fits the description of the ideal mate you've created on that list. While they may not meet all the criteria on your list, you will want to make sure that they fit all the things that are truly important to you. For instance let's say your list consists of the following: tall, brown skinned, pretty smile, white teeth, smart, goes to church, respects his elders, doesn't get into trouble in school, plays football, reads his Bible regularly, doesn't curse, and is honest. Perhaps you meet a guy and he possesses all the above except he doesn't have white teeth and doesn't play football. Does the fact that he doesn't have white teeth and he doesn't play football really matter in the grand scheme of things? Not at all. He appears to possess all the characteristics that really matter. This is what I mean by a guy may not have all the attributes you want, but does he have the things that really matter in the long run? I refer you back to what I said in an earlier chapter about being beautiful on the outside, but having a mean spirit or deceitful heart on the inside. Guys can be the same way. A guy may have all the physical attributes you could ever want in a guy, and be missing so much of what is necessary to make him a good-hearted person. Choose your boyfriends carefully.

Another aspect of relationships is choosing to be with someone who wants to be with you. You should not go out there looking for a boyfriend and you certainly shouldn't be with someone that has not first expressed a clear interest in you and only you. That's right, if you meet a guy who is in a relationship with someone else, but says he is interested in you, you need to give him time to resolve and dissolve that current relationship before he starts dating you. Don't fall for the mindset of those who say, "If his girlfriend were doing her job, he wouldn't even be looking in my direction." While this may be true in some instances, most of the time it's not true and you should not fall for it. If his girlfriend isn't doing her job, then maybe he should be smart and leave her alone. Regardless, you should allow him time to leave that relationship before getting involved with him.

It's not cute to go around "stealing" another girl's boyfriend, nor is it cute to go around bragging about it. Think about it this way, if he is able to be stolen from someone else, don't you think someone could steal him from you.

There is an old saying that states, "You will lose a man the same way you got him." That in turn means, if you stole him, he'll be stolen from you. Watch out for guys that are in relationships and want to get involved with you. You may be setting yourself up for a real heartbreak. Have respect for yourself and make him come to you the right way. You will feel much better about yourself knowing that you weren't the cause of another girl being hurt and you didn't settle for someone that you had to "take" from someone else. Respect yourself and others will respect you. Also remember, you reap what you sow. Meaning, if you take someone else's man, someone will eventually take yours. Maybe even the one you stole! It won't feel so good when it happens to you, nor will it be something to brag to your friends about.

Let me address the whole issue around fighting over "your man." There isn't a site more troubling for me to see when it comes to women, than seeing them fight over a guy. Fighting verbally and physically over a guy is unattractive and embarrassing, especially in public. You might not think so at the time, but really now, do you want to go down in history known as the girl who fought over her man? I would hope not. Let me give you some reasons why it's not a good idea to fight over a boyfriend. First of all, you could get hurt or permanently scarred in the fight. Long after your relationship has ended, you'll still be wearing the battle scars, but not the man. You may also be fighting a young woman over a lie that he may have told one or both of you in order for him to get what he wanted from you both. You could get kicked out of school or even arrested for brawling in public. How cute would a mug shot of you be? Oh and don't forget the court fees and the new criminal record you'll have which may prohibit you from getting a job or getting into college. Lastly, it's not a good idea to fight over your man because if you are at the point where you are in a situation where a fight is even considered, then he's probably not worth it. Really! Be a class act and take the high road, someone more deserving of your time will come along, and you'll be much happier that you didn't stoop to the level of brawling over a guy.

If you meet a guy, and he is in a relationship, he is UNAVAILABLE. He is unavailable to be in a relationship with you. If you want to be with a guy who is smart, but a guy is telling you he is in a relationship where he is unhappy, then he's not acting very smart, is he? If he were smart, then he'd respect himself and get out of something that was draining him of his happiness. Chances are he's not being honest with you, and he wants to have his cake and eat it too. Don't fall for all the wonderful things he's saying, just move on. He is not worth your time, and you shouldn't give it to him.

Let's just say, he is unhappy, and he's trying to get out of a relationship slowly as to not break the other girl's heart too badly. If this is the case, respect him for what he's trying to do, and let him know that you may be available once he's cut his ties with her. Staying out of the way while he works through his relationship is in your best interest. You are protecting your own feelings by doing so. Waiting is the best option for you because you don't want to get ahead of the game and find yourself heartbroken because he chose to stay with her after all.

Before I got married, I use to have a rule when I was dating. That rule was: I would not date a guy that had recently gotten out of a relationship within the past six months to a year. This was in an effort to safeguard my heart against any residual feelings he may have had for his ex after they'd broken up. If six months to a year had gone by, and he had not felt the need to restore or rekindle the previous relationship, then I deemed him available for me to date. This is not a foolproof system for dating, but it worked for me most of the time.

You deserve to be in a relationship with someone who wants to be with you and only you; someone who respects you and has your best interest at heart; someone who has no desire to cheat on you; and someone who can be honest with you. If you are with someone that does not fit the above, please end it before you wind up regretting you ever met that person.

On the issue of sex, where do I begin? Well, the Bible tells us that sex outside of marriage is wrong and refers to sex before marriage as *fornication*. I'm sure you have heard that word before. So first of all, I doubt you are married if you are reading this book; and secondly, I would guess that you are in high school. Thirdly, if you're not in high school and you're not married, then this applies to you as well. Other than the fact God said it is wrong and we shouldn't do it, let's talk about some other reasons why it's not a good idea to have sex with your boyfriend.

I'm sure you have learned about all the sexually transmitted diseases. Yes, of course you subject yourselves to various infections when you are having sex with various partners. You may be saying, "I don't sleep around," or "I've been with my boyfriend for a long time, and he's the only one." While that may be true at the moment, if you are not married to him, then there is always that chance you could break up, and you'll get a new boyfriend. Then your sex life starts all over again. So essentially you can have multiple partners even if it's not at the same time. Also keep in mind that you are having sex with all the other girls your partner has ever had sex with. Taking precautions or practicing "safe sex" is not enough of a safeguard. Abstinence is really the only way you guard yourself against STD's.

Abstinence is also the way you protect yourself from a devastating heartbreak. Let me explain what I mean. When you are involved with someone sexually, you are creating a bond with that person. This sexual bond along with the strong emotional feelings you have for that person connects you to them in a way that requires a certain level of maturity that a young woman such as yourself may not have. You're right, I don't know you personally, but I do know that at your developmental stage, you are not ready for the emotional weight that a sexual relationship carries. I actually know adult women who can't handle the emotional weight of a sexual relationship.

If you don't believe me, think about it this way. When a person is involved in a relationship (notice I said relationship, not just someone sleeping around) where sex is involved, and then the relationship ends, their behavior is markedly different than if there is no sex involved. Sure, the ending of any relationship can create a certain amount of sadness, tears, and sometimes anger, but in my experience when sex is involved those emotions were magnified times two. For example, after breaking up with your boyfriend who you've been dating for 8 months (and there was sex), you are more likely to become enraged when you find him dating someone new. Notice I said enraged, not just mad. You may even find yourself unable to let go even if several weeks have passed since the breakup. Other uncontrollable displays of emotions could range anywhere from stalking him and his new girlfriend to finding a new boyfriend immediately to replace him, which is very irrational and not recommended. Someone else going through a breakup where sex *was not* involved may still feel hurt by the breakup, but would tend to resolve their feelings faster and be less likely to act in such a way that is out of control or out of character for them.

The point I want to make is that involving sex in a relationship is not just about being careful and protecting yourself against STD's, but also protecting yourself against emotional turmoil that you are not ready to handle. There is a reason God forbids us from engaging in sex outside of marriage. He loves us and is trying to protect us from what he knows will be devastating should we have to endure the negative side of it. Think long and hard before you have sex with your boyfriend. You're not ready emotionally, and it could take you a very long time to recover from a breakup.

Relationships can take weird turns at times and often right before your eyes without you even realizing what is going on. If you find yourself in a relationship where you feel you are not being respected, you feel you're being abused verbally or physically, you feel you are being cheated on or lied to constantly, get out immediately and preserve your self respect. Your boyfriend may encourage you to stay and work things out with him and not break up. He may tell you he will change or not do "it" again. He may even tell you that if you break up with him no one else is going to want you. Take your chances to see if someone else will want you, especially if he's not treating the way you should be treated, which in turn says he doesn't want you. At least one thing is clear, he doesn't want you because if he did he'd treat you better. Get out and get moving. The situation will only get worse with time. Unless this young man has a spiritual intervention and turns his life over to God, he will continue to hurt you, and one day it could be fatal. Even if you don't end up physically hurt, you could end up emotionally drained, depressed, and sad, possibly leaving you bitter and resentful as I mentioned previously. Don't waste your time or put yourself in harm's way for what you imagine to be love. When you are loved by someone, you can be very clear on what that looks like by reading and meditating over 1 Corinthians 13:4-7. I quote these verses below for your reference. I love this passage and what it says so much that I want to share it here with you.

Love is patient, love is kind. It does not envy, it does not boast, it is not proud. It is not rude, it is not self-seeking, it is not easily angered, it keeps no record of wrongs.

Love does not delight in evil but rejoices with the truth. It always protects, always trusts, always hopes, always perseveres (NIV).

This description of love in 1 Corinthians is what real, Godly love should look like in your life regardless of the type of relationship you are involved in. This is a Godly type of love that should serve as an example to all.

Notes

Chapter 11:
Who Can You Turn to
When Your Relationship Is in Trouble?

The answer to this question is not easy, but you want to first make sure you choose someone you can trust. You may feel uncomfortable sharing your relationship problems with your parents, but remember, your parents love you and want the best for you and would probably do anything to protect you. I know sometimes sharing your relationship problems with your parents or other family members could result in them not liking your boyfriend and forbid him from coming around. While you may want to protect him against negative treatment by your family, just think of how he may be treating you. You must first determine the severity of what you may consider a "problem." If you and your boyfriend are having arguments or disagreements about things, and you are able to resolve the disagreement without staying mad with each other for more than two days, or if your disagreements do not *ever* lead to physical or heated verbal altercations, then it may not be necessary to involve your parents or other family members in the situation. However, if the opposite occurs, then letting your parents in on what's going on is crucial.

By involving your parents you are doing two things. You are allowing them firsthand knowledge about what's going on so they can protect you, and you are serving notice to this so-called boyfriend that someone knows what he is doing and will hold him accountable. Even if he decides to break up with you, it is his loss and your gain. You certainly don't need someone in your life that wants to hurt you, and furthermore someone who has a problem being held accountable for his actions. You'll gain in this situation by keeping your dignity as well as your self-esteem intact.

If for whatever reason you may feel that it is impossible to go to your parents or a family member when your relationship goes sour, find someone that you can trust that has some authority. This does not mean your best friend who is probably too young to help. Choose to talk with a school counselor, a police officer, the youth pastor or youth leader at your church, a family friend, a close neighbor, or any other trusted adult.

I know you want to think you are old enough to handle your own business, and you don't feel the need to tell anyone what's going on with you, but keeping secrets like abuse only hurts you in the long run. While broadcasting your business to the world is not a good idea, sharing it with someone you trust is. Crying silently and alone about the pain you may be going through is not healthy; talking about your pain can be the first steps to your healing.

I wish to offer one word of caution here: Don't confuse love with sex; it's not the same thing! If you are having sex (and you shouldn't be) don't think this person loves you or is in love with you just because you are having sex. Love and sex do not necessarily go hand in hand.

Someone may say they love you so they can have sex with you. Please don't fall for that old line. If they love you, then they should be willing to wait until you are ready to make such a huge life choice, preferably on your wedding night. However, if waiting until your wedding night is not realistic for you, then certainly wait until you are emotionally ready to handle the possible rejection that may come after sleeping with someone too soon after you've become involved with them. High school is usually not the time you are emotionally ready for this type of relationship.

Another aspect of dating involves understanding when a relationship is over. When the guy you have been involved with has ended the relationship, walk away gracefully and with dignity. Regardless of whether he has become involved with someone else or not, when it's over, it's over. It is not a pleasant sight to observe someone crying hysterically and making a public scene over a break-up.

When relationships end, they can sometimes stir up sad emotions. This reaction is normal and expected in most situations, especially for young women your age. However, the reactions that are not normal and often lead to other problems include stalking him, calling him on his cell phone or home phone repeatedly (harassment), calling his new girlfriend, best friends, his family members (especially his mother), breaking out the headlights on his car, slashing his tires, or spreading rumors about him. His mother may really like you and wish the two of you had not broken up, but the reality is, his mother does not choose his girlfriends for him, and she cannot make him date you if he has decided he doesn't want to. The other behaviors mentioned can get you into serious trouble with the law.

The best thing for you to do is accept his decision to end the relationship and move on. You will get over him, trust me. A break-up is sometimes very hard to cope with at first. You may feel sad about not having him around or not having him to call or take you to the movies, etc. But guess what? He may have been the first, but he sure won't be the last. You may be saying, "That's easier said than done, I love him," and I'm sure you do; but crying won't make him come back. Actually all crying will do is give you a very bad headache and make your eyes a little puffy, and then everyone will know you've been crying. While crying sometimes is helpful in allowing you to release some of those painful emotions, you don't want to become stuck in that place. Cry and keep moving ahead.

The point I am strongly trying to make here is that acting out in public over your breakup draws negative attention to you, not your man. Cursing him out in public may make you feel better and that you've gotten the best of him, but in reality, it makes you look stupid in the public eye. What people will really being saying is, "She looks like someone who can't get over losing her man," not, "He's a jerk for breaking up with her."

Public displays of anger in the form of aggressive behavior (verbal or physical), is not a mature reaction and is a turnoff to most people. People may laugh at the scene and talk about it later, but they will not be speaking pleasantly about you. Besides, ask yourself, "Do I want to be remembered as the girl that got dumped and acted like a fool in public about it." If your answer is "no," then reserve any reaction or comment for your ex when you can speak with him privately. At the end of the day, it's nobody's business what goes on in your relationship. Say what you have to say privately, and move on. Don't waste any time on someone who has said they are no longer interested in being with you. Trust me, it's not cute to try to hang on to a man that doesn't want you. You are beautiful and strong inside and out; someone will see the diamond in you, even if it's not him.

If by some chance he realizes he made a mistake and wants to date you again, for your sake, don't be so quick to get back with him. After all, he did dump you. Take some time to think about your relationship and where things went wrong. It's ok to stay broken up for longer than a few days to make sure that he's really worth getting back involved with. Try not to rush to take him back just because he has apologized for his wrongdoing or because you fear if you wait too long, he may not want to get back together so you better act now. If taking some time is not acceptable to him, and he's pressuring you to make a decision, then take that as a sign and move on without him. Oftentimes, the person who makes the mistake of hurting their girlfriend or boyfriend wants to be forgiven immediately with everything forgotten and get back to the way things were before. They often don't want to talk about what caused the break-up or deal with a problem once it's brought to light. They want you to forget the drama ever happened, and accept them back and be happy. Wrong, your job is to take as long as you need to work through any concerns you may have, ask any questions you need, and make the right decision for you!

Now, on the flip side, if you are the one who broke up with him, make sure you don't take him on a roller coaster ride. If you go as far as to break up with him, there was obviously a reason for that decision. Try not to create in your life what I call the "revolving door." The revolving door is the one that keeps allowing the same people to be recycled in and out of your life, over and over again. You can control this. If you break up with someone, think long and hard before you take him back. Remember, he is an ex-boyfriend for a reason. Being strung along is hurtful to anyone, including guys. So if you are doing the stringing along of someone you really don't want to be with, stop it right now.

Dating or being in a relationship with someone can and should be fun and exciting, but you don't have to be in a rush to go there just because most or all your friends are doing it. While being in a relationship is exciting, so can being single or hanging with your girlfriends. Being single and not involved in a relationship is an opportunity for you to discover who you are and understand why you make the decisions you make. It also gives you time to focus on yourself and build on your strengths as well as work on areas that are more challenging for you.

You will have plenty opportunities to date; so instead of feeling left out when most of your friends have boyfriends, try seeing yourself in a different perspective, one that allows you to see yourself as an individual and not part of a couple. Take time to commune with God and understand his purpose for your life. After you get a clear perspective, find some answers and learn to love and care for yourself inside and out, you will be better equipped to successfully handle a relationship when it finally comes.

For some of you wanting to be in a relationship right now, but aren't, it might not be the right time for you. It doesn't mean you aren't attractive enough, smart enough or good enough. Don't dwell on those things; focus on doing all you can to better yourself. Don't go out looking for a guy to date, let the guys find you. This way you'll know he's interested in you because he sought you out, not because you approached him.

Many of you reading this section may not be at the point in your life where you are dating seriously, or dating at all yet. That doesn't mean these words don't apply to you. You may not be able to relate directly, but remember what you are reading so when you do start to date, you don't succumb to the pitfalls of what could be an unhealthy relationship.

Remember, if you find yourself in a situation with a guy that has gotten out of control in any way, whether he's hurting you verbally, physically or emotionally, or you are the one that is being the aggressor, you should consider your relationship in trouble. This kind of trouble requires getting your parents or another trusted adult involved. Anger and abuse can go hand in hand in relationships, so make sure you have someone in your life you can turn to if things should head for trouble. Keep in mind, someone intervening early into an unhealthy and unstable situation, could save yours or his life. Abuse of any kind is unhealthy and unacceptable.

Notes

Chapter 12:
Friendships

"A man(woman) that hath friends must shew himself friendly: and there is a friend that sticketh closer than a brother (sister)" (Proverbs 18:24, KJV).

Friendships are relationships, and they are important for us to have in our lives. Healthy ones can bring us lots of joy and great memories. I often hear girls say they don't get along with other girls and tend to get along with guys better. This may really be the case for some of those girls who say that, but for others it is merely a cop-out used to keep from forming bonds with other women for whatever reason.

Jealousy may be one of those reasons. As women, it is easy for us to become jealous of another woman because of the way she looks, her hair length, her shape, the way she dresses, the way she speaks, the fact that men find her attractive, etc. Jealously is unbecoming and is quite a turn-off for men as well as women. The Bible has this to say about jealousy, *"Let us not become conceited, provoking and envying each other"* (Gal 5:26, NIV).

There is much we can learn from each other as women if we give each other a chance. Friendships are priceless. Making friends is not hard although it may seem difficult if you are not a very outgoing person. Even if you are not outgoing, you can still make friends and have great friends in your circle. In order to have a friend, you must be a friend, so show yourself to be friendly. To begin cultivating friendships, you may want to try to present yourself as friendly with a smile, a handshake upon meeting someone, a kind expression on your face, or a shared laugh. These are all ways that let others know you are friendly and approachable. Things that can turn a potential friend off are a frown on your face, a reputation of being a gossiper, always sitting alone, turning up your nose at people, or holding your head down. You certainly want to appear approachable to people if you expect them to approach you or want to be around you.

To cultivate friendships, first start with showing yourself friendly, then move on to employing the elements necessary to maintain a healthy relationship.

Ask yourself, "What do I need in a friend? What do I want in a friend? What am I willing to do to have a friend?" None of your answers to these questions should involve compromising your self respect, integrity, or dignity in any way.

Instead of being jealous or envious of your friends, try supporting them when they do something good, or compliment them when they get a new car or outfit. Try encouraging them when they are trying out for cheerleading, track, or basketball, even if you're not trying out. Try giving words of comfort when they break up with their boyfriends instead of being happy that they are now alone too, or that they no longer have the *hot* guy in school. Try telling *them* how you feel about them, even if it's not a nice feeling or opinion, rather than going behind their back and telling your other friends how you feel about a particular friend. Support your friends when you believe in them, tell them you believe in them and that you support what they are doing. When you give love, love will come back to you. The Bible refers to this principal as "reaping and sowing." When you sow seeds of love, support, and encouragement toward others, you reap those same things in return. The Bible says ***Do not be deceived: God cannot be mocked. A man reaps what he sows*** (Gal 6:7, NIV). Keep this verse in mind especially if you ever feel like sowing something negative. First of all you can surely expect the negativity to come back to you, and secondly, you can't truly call yourself a friend, not with a heart like this.

Jealousy and envy have caused many friendships to break up. Jealousy and envy are poisonous and deadly to any relationship. Oftentimes you may not be able to recognize jealousy for what it is. A jealous person may not even see how bad their jealousy really is. If you or your friends carry jealousy as a character flaw, ask God to remove it from your heart (because that's where jealousy lives) and replace it with love and acceptance for others.

Friendships are great bonds that tend to grow stronger daily; but always keep in mind that you are an individual first and then a friend. You are an individual that is still responsible for her own choices, attitudes, and behaviors. When you think of your *girls* or your girlfriends, you probably think of the closeness you share, the secrets you share, the laughter, and the tears. It's a wonderful feeling to have friends you can share those things with, especially your girlfriends. While you and your girlfriends may even share some of the same enemies, it's not cool to become enemies with a girl just because she's your friend's enemy. Sometimes girls have issues with other girls, and that is to be expected, but if your girlfriend has an issue with another young woman that doesn't involve you, then it's her issue and hers alone. Don't dislike another person just because your friend dislikes her. If anything, maybe you could encourage your friend to drop her beef with this person, be the bigger, classier person and move on or let it go. You could also express to your friend that you feel it's unbecoming and a turnoff, not to mention pointless to hold on to grudges. Even though she may feel justified in her actions, she still doesn't have the upper hand, why? Because the energy your friend uses to dislike this person is being wasted and could be used for something more beneficial in her life. And guess what; if you dislike this person too, then you are wasting that same energy? You are too bright for that. It's ok if you don't want to be friends with someone or dislike someone's behavior, but staging a campaign against them is not cool and a waste of your valuable time.

Always remember the differences between healthy and unhealthy relationships and make sure that all your relationships are healthy. Some key things to remember are: Verbal, emotional, and physical abuse is not okay and you don't have to stay around someone who treats you in ways that don't feel good to you. A healthy friendship will not require you to lower your standards and act in a way that goes against what you know to be right.

Notes

College/Career

Chapter 13:
College and
Career Choices

For even when we were with you, we gave you this rule: "If a man [woman] will not work, he [she] shall not eat" (2 Thess 3:20).

You may or may not be at a point yet in your life where college and a career are in your near future, but you will soon get there. You should be thinking about the next phase of your life which will ultimately require you to make a decision about how you will support yourself. The above scripture clearly states that if you don't work, you don't eat. Think about if for a minute, if you are able to work, shouldn't you work? And if you don't work, should you really be able to eat? Of course you are not being required to completely care for yourself at this time, but looking ahead will certainly make it easier to transition into college or a career when you do need to work to support yourself.

What do you want to do with your life? Where will you be attending college? Will you attend college? How will you support yourself after you leave high school? Will you be going to the military or attending a vocational school? These are all questions that I am sure you have either already been asked or will likely be asked over the next few years. And yes, you should have an answer for each of them. You may not have the answer that most people in your life would like to hear, but you need to have given some thought to these questions beforehand. Spend some time thinking about how you will get to the next level in life and what steps you plan to take to accomplish your goals after high school.

Everyone will not go to college, and everyone is not expected to go to college, but now is the time for you to start thinking about your future. Even if you say today you want to become a doctor and make plans to become a doctor, but down the line change your mind, at least you had a plan. Having a plan is the focus here. Create a plan for your future and have it be your roadmap to success.

It's expected that over the course of five to ten years, you may change your mind about what you want to do in life several times. The fact that you may change your mind about your career goals is not an excuse not to make plans. Why? Because having a plan is a way to help you stay focused and on track. Having a plan doesn't mean you have to do everything you say you are going to do, but you will at least have a good idea of where you are headed. Take going on a trip for example. If you plan to go to Florida, and you've never been there before, you are likely to get a map. While you are on your way to Florida, you may stop at many destinations, some planned and unplanned, but you are on the right track and have some specific stops in mind. On the other hand what if you didn't have a map or any idea of where Florida is? It is likely that you will spend a lot of time at places you didn't plan to go, spending money you didn't plan to spend, and wasting a lot of time that you really don't have. The same situation can occur when you get caught without a plan for your life.

Keep in mind, all of your plans may not come to fruition, but that is not what setting goals is all about. What situation would you rather be in, having a set of goals to follow and coming close to accomplishing those goals, or not having a set of goals at all and feeling out of place and not sure of what your next move will be? Go ahead and make plans.

Notes

Chapter 14:
Let's Talk about Setting Goals

As you may know by now, the purpose of setting goals is to have a road-map for your life that will guide you down the paths that lead you to your own desired destination. Sure, you can happen into success or even happen into a good *situation*, as many people have done. It is not however, the recommended approach. I recommend sitting down and planning out your life as you would a date with friends or a trip with your family.

I'd like to note here that just because you make plans, things may not al-ways go according to those plans, because *life happens*. What do I mean by that? Well, let's say while you are in the eleventh grade you make plans to go to college, and your family has saved a lot of money for you to go to college. Then one day your father gets news that his employer is laying him off. Over the next several months, he's unable to find a job and when he does find one, it doesn't pay nearly the amount of money he was making with his previous job. In addition, during the months he was unemployed, your father had to dip into family savings as well as the money your family had been saving for you to go to college. Your plans for going to college have now been altered due to monetary constraints. This doesn't mean you can't go to college, it just means something unforeseen has happened and your plans have been altered. In this situation, as with most, a plan "B" needs to already be in place so that very little time is lost.

I am not encouraging you to plan every aspect of your life. Planning every aspect of your life is not realistic anyway. I don't want you to be rigid in your goal setting either, because I don't want you to feel overwhelmed when something doesn't go as you planned. The big picture is to have a plan for where you want to go and what you want to do with your life. If you miss, but get close, then you have essentially hit the mark.

You may be thinking, "What if I don't see tomorrow or live for ten more years, what's the point of setting long-term goals?" Isn't there a scripture that tells us to not make plans for tomorrow, but to let tomorrow take care of itself? Well actually that scripture is at Matthew 6:34 and what it says is: ***Therefore do not worry about tomorrow, for tomorrow will worry about itself. Each day has enough trouble of its own*** (NIV). The point being made by Matthew is you shouldn't *worry* about tomorrow. God doesn't want us worrying about anything; however he doesn't say we shouldn't *plan* for tomorrow.

Goal Setting

Ask yourself, what do I want to do, where do I want to go, how will I get there, how will I know that I have achieved my goals beyond the obvious? Your goals must be measurable and time-sensitive.

When setting goals, make sure they are attainable. For example, don't set a goal to become a professional athlete just because you like to play basketball, and you think it would be cool. If you have not placed yourself in the right environment, met the right people, played high school basketball, or gotten yourself in top physical shape, this may not be a goal that is realistic or attainable. Of course, my belief is that you can accomplish anything you set your mind on and are committed to, but isn't it unrealistic to strive for something that you have not been preparing for or actually expect to happen. My point here is, be realistic in setting your goals.

On the other hand, don't just set goals that you know you can achieve easily without any effort. While easily achieved goals should not be discounted, you should also set goals that will require hard work and effort. You've probably heard the saying, "Anything worth having is worth the hard work." I believe this to be true in a lot of cases. In my personal experience, the things I've done in my life that I appreciate the most and feel most proud of are the things I worked hard for and put my very best foot forward to achieve. For example, completing my undergraduate and master's degrees, both of which I worked extremely hard for, didn't come easy for me. I worked fulltime during graduate school and never missed a beat. I was often tired and overwhelmed at all I had to do, but I kept the bigger picture (graduation) in mind and kept pressing on even harder. Not only did I receive my degrees as I had intended, but I felt proud of it because I knew the hard work and effort I put into doing it, better than anyone else knew.

This doesn't mean I am not appreciative of the things I didn't work as hard for because I am grateful for those things as well, it just means I appreciate *more* the things I gave a greater effort to accomplishing.

Start your goal setting by making short-term and long-term goals. Short-term goals are goals you want to accomplish within one to two years. Long-term goals are goals you want to accomplish in more than two years. Long-term goals can even be goals you want to accomplish in the next ten years.

Write out each goal. Underneath each goal, write out when you want to have it completed (by what age or what year), and how you plan to reach it. Look at the example below.

Short-term goal: Graduate from college on time

- Graduation year 2011
- I plan to graduate on time by taking all required coursework and no less than 15 hours a semester.
  * Speak with advisor on a quarterly basis to make sure I stay on track and up to date with any school policy changes
  * Make no less than a "C" in all my classes
  * Do not drop any classes if I can help it
- Enroll in summer school if necessary to keep me on track

If you look at the example on the previous, you can see that the goal has been set, a timeframe for completion has been established, and a plan of action to follow in order to get there has been determined. Following this goal setting outline does two things: 1) you put the goal on paper; (putting things on paper helps better commit them to memory); and 2) writing out your goal and plan to achieve it gives you something to refer back to on a regular basis to determine how close you've come to reaching your goal and allows you to see if you have a lot of work still left to do in accomplishing that particular goal.

I recommend reviewing your goal sheet at least two to three times per year. Keep it somewhere that you can easily get to it. This is not just an exercise for you as a teenager who's planning out her life. This is a practice you can employ even in your adult life. I still set goals for myself in my personal life, as well as my professional life.

As you get older, your goals are likely to change or you will create new ones as you begin to accomplish the ones you've already set. Creating a roadmap by setting goals is a good way to help you stay on track with what you intend to do.

Notes

Chapter 15:
Research

Another very important aspect of planning for your future is to do research. I can't stress enough how important it is to research any important decision in your life. Pulling together the necessary information to lead you to your dream is vitally important. Why? There are many types of careers that exist that you may not even be aware of. We are most familiar with the popular ones like lawyers, doctors, hairstylist, engineers, salespersons, police officers, secretaries, athletes, teachers, nurses, etc., but there are many more that you may not have heard of and may actually find interesting if you knew about them.

That is not to say that the popular ones should not be considered. If you have not already determined what you want to do (or even if you have), it may not be a bad idea to look into the various types of careers that exist. Your guidance counselor at your school should be able to provide you with information on various types of careers as well as the skills required to perform those professions or trades. There are even tools available to help you determine areas that you may be better suited for than the one you have chosen. Check with your counselor to find out what types of resources your school has for you to look at.

When you are researching different careers or jobs, make sure you are also looking for things like pay range, companies who employ those positions, areas of the country most likely in need for those positions, educational requirements, previous experience requirements, and if future certifications or licensing will be necessary. These are just a few suggestions of what your career research should include.

Find out all you can about the careers you are interested in by looking through various books available through your guidance office or career office, if you are in college. Check out books from the library or purchase career books from the bookstore to help in your research. Take a look at business magazines available in your local bookstore. Also, if you happen to know someone already in a career you think you might be interested in pursuing, speak with that person candidly about their experience in that field and the ups and downs they may have experienced.

Researching is by far the best way to help you assess the careers in which you are interested. Some people know from a very young age what they'd like to do for a living; others don't decide until later. So if you have not already decided, spend some time researching what you'd like to do.

As you begin to research, keep in mind the things you are particularly good at, the things you like to do and get the most joy and pleasure out of doing, and things you could actually see yourself doing for a very long time. You may know people who say they got stuck in a career or job that they hate or are not happy doing. Some of these people may have ended up in a particular job because that was all that was available to them at the time, or they may not have done thorough research to guide them into a great job opportunity. There may have also been a lack of planning/goal-setting on their part; and left without a plan, you could end up anywhere. You may also hear those same individuals or others say things like, "If I had to do it all over again, I would do things differently, or go to school, or go to college, or wait to have children, etc." Listen to those adults and take heed because they are giving you loads of advice in those statements alone.

After you have determined the jobs you feel you might be good at and would like to pursue and you have completed your research, be prepared! As you begin to meet people (and it's never too early and you are never too young to network), always be prepared to get their phone numbers or give yours. Provide them with a copy of your resume. Even if you don't have one on you at the time you meet them, let them know you will get one to them the next day. The only way you can actually get them a good copy of your resume the next day is if you already have one on your computer. Don't promise something you cannot make good on. This could have a negative impact on any future opportunities. So make sure you have a resume prepared and on your computer. Don't feel intimidated if you don't have any formal work experience; very little experience is expected at your age. But remember, it is okay to provide any information about any type of work you have done and any skills you may have. Those work experiences and skills could include babysitting children or animals, cleaning house, computer word processing knowledge, filing, getting things organized, etc.

You should make yourself aware of any job or career fairs in your area. You should also consider joining any organizations that provide networking opportunities. These organizations could be anything from Habitat for Humanity and Four H Club to Greek organizations and Future Business Leaders of America. Not only will these organizations provide networking opportunities, but some will allow you the opportunity to give back to the community in various ways through volunteering your time. Volunteering is very important and helpful when filling out applications for colleges.

In stressing the importance of being prepared, it is not a good idea to attend any event, function, or meeting *half cocked*. Always bring your "A" game. Putting your best foot forward is sometimes the thing that sets you apart from another person, especially in job selection.

When you are looking for a job, more than likely most of the people that get pass the application process and make it to the interview are qualified for the job. So I would say that at this point in the process, you all are on the same playing field. This is where you must shine. You must come to your interview with the attitude that you are the right person for the job; then sell that attitude to your interviewer.

Throughout my career I have had the opportunity to interview candidates for jobs. Some of the things I saw during that process concerned me greatly. Lack of preparation was one of the biggest issues I found. When you are not prepared, the right question can throw you completely off and cause the interview to go bad quickly. What's even worse, the interviewer will be able to see that you are not prepared by the way you answer their questions.

Interviewing Skills

There will come a time when you will have to interview for a job. It is very important that you establish good interviewing skills. Learning how to interview well can mean the difference between getting the job or not getting the job.

The interview process starts long before you sit down in front of the interviewer. It begins with learning as much as you can about the company and the way they do business.

For example, everyone knows McDonald's sells hamburgers and French fries, so giving the interviewer that information is not likely to impress. If you were to tell the interviewer something about how McDonald's got started or who their founder was, or even something about what they do in the community, you are more likely to impress the interviewer with this information. They will already know this information, but making this information a part of your interview will tell them that you have done your homework about the company and can be seen as someone who will go above and beyond what is required.

Why is this important? Employers want to know that when they hire someone, that person will be a hard worker, dedicated to what they are doing, and willing to do a little more than the minimum required. Employers want to invest in someone who has shown these characteristics. If you possess these characteristics it is likely that you will be strongly considered for the job. Doing a little more than the minimum required says that you are ambitious and you are driven. Wouldn't you want this kind of person on your team?

Below are some interview tips to help you through the interview process. I encourage you to use them as you begin your job search. You are never too young to start learning this process.

Tips on Interviewing
(Getting the job)
✓ **Research the company.** Find out important facts about the company and write them down. Bring them up in the interview when the opportunity arises. This shows the interviewer that you've done your homework.

✓ **Be on time.** Arrive at least 15 minutes before your scheduled interview.
  - Use this extra time to take a deep breath, fix your clothes/makeup, comb hair and go over your notes.

✓ **Use good eye contact.** Look the interviewer in the eyes when you are speaking. Looking away often may give them the wrong impression.

✓ **Do not chew gum.**

✓ **Do not bring your cell phone in the interview room with you.** If you do not have anyplace to leave it, make sure you turn it OFF!

✓ **Do not bring friends or relatives to the interview with you.** And definitely don't bring them in the interview room with you. If someone drives you to the interview, ask them to drop you off and come back later, or have them wait in the parking lot (with the music turned down really low). They really should not come inside the building with you.

✓ **Don't get too personal.** Answer the questions in detail that are asked, but be careful to not talk about your personal life if it doesn't relate to the job you are applying for.

✓ **Give detailed responses.** One word answers can be seen as having a limited vocabulary.

✓ **Smile and be pleasant to everyone you come in contact with at the company.** This includes the person answering the phone or giving you the application and other people in the waiting area, etc. This is very important because you never know how these people can impact your chance of getting the job. If you are rude or nasty to someone before you get inside the interview room, that person may remember your behavior and let the interviewer know about it.

✓ **Wear clothing that is appropriate.**
  - no skirts above mid thigh
  - please don't show your cleavage
  - clothing that reveals your curves or is too tight is inappropriate
  - clothing that is colorful, but not loud in presentation is appropriate

✓ **If you must wear cologne or scented body lotion, keep it to a minimum.** Everyone does not like the same scents and some people could be allergic to them. So keep this in mind and remember, a minimum if you must!

Once you have chosen your career path, you are well on your way to being committed to a particular employment field. Whatever it is you decide to do, see it through. Don't give up because you encounter aspects of your job that may feel too challenging or overwhelming. Always put your best into every project or assignment, so at the end of the day, you can say you gave it your all. This is actually a practice that you could use in every aspect of your life, job, relationships, school, sports, etc. If you walk away from something after you have done the best you could do, then you walk free of regrets, "wouldas" and "shouldas."

Notes

Chapter 16:
Habits of Excellence

Giving your best to something means preparedness; it also means training yourself in habits of excellence. Below is a list of those habits of excellence that you should make a part of your life in all that you do.

1. **Pray daily** – find the time to commune with the Lord to give thanks and praise, ask for forgiveness when you have done wrong, and ask for guidance.

2. **Practice honesty** – it keeps you above board on all your dealings with people and the respect you will receive because of your honest dealings is immeasurable.

3. **Practice kindness** – it won't hurt you to be kind to another; actually God requires it of us.

4. **Develop a good work ethic** – be on time, learn your job to the fullest, do your best at it and don't cheat your employer.

5. **Always be prepared** – don't allow yourself to be caught off-guard.

6. **Read, Read, Read!** – reading builds knowledge and knowledge is power.

7. **Be a visionary** – don't always take things at face value or look at the current state, look ahead at what things could look like or how things could be.

8. **Meditate on God's word** – read the Bible daily and allow yourself time to digest what you are reading, then figure out how it can apply to what is going on in your life or your world at that particular time, then use it to be a better person or to help someone that may need it.

9. **Stay in order** – the Bible says ***Let all things be done decently and in order*** (1Cor 14:40, NIV). Order simply means "regular arrangement." Don't allow yourself to get out of place when it comes to your role in the workplace, your role at home or your role at school. It also means that if you have a certain plan to follow, make it a practice to follow the plan accordingly. Try not to put the cart before the horse, so to speak. Because we all know the cart doesn't pull the horse; the horse pulls the cart. An orderly life tends to run a little smoother than one filled with chaos and confusion. In terms of being decent, well that almost goes without saying, but I will speak to it anyway. You should always practice being decent in all your dealings. This means to exhibit appropriate, clean behavior and to speak with a positive tongue, not a foul one.

One way to keep yourself in check and know if you are on the right track is to ask yourself often if your behavior the day before shames you, makes you feel bad or embarrassed, or actually makes you feel good about what you did the day before.

Notes

Chapter 17:
Financial Planning
and Budgeting

Most young women your age are probably not thinking about financial planning, but you should be. Even if you don't have a job or make any money, it's not a bad idea to get into the mindset of thinking about what you would like to do with the money you make. Just because you make the money, doesn't mean you have to spend it all. That's where savings comes into play. Please do not forget to tithe. The Bible talks about being good stewards (responsible agents) over the things which we have been blessed or given responsibility (read Luke 16:1-12, The Parable of the Shrewd Manager.) Responsibility over things includes money. In verse 10 of Luke 16 it goes on to say, *Whoever can be trusted with very little can also be trusted with much, and whoever is dishonest with very little, will also be dishonest with much.*

Whenever you get paid, you should first practice setting aside ten percent of what you earn as your tithe, that portion of your pay which you will give back to God for his blessing of a job that allows you to make money. Not only is this a practice you should put into place, but it is required of you according to the word of God (see Mal 3:10). Tithing is about being obedient to the word of God.

Many of you reading this book may already be tithing in your churches or wherever you may worship, and that is excellent! Some of you may be saying, "What if I don't attend church or don't have a job where I make money?" If you don't attend church, you can still find a church that you would like to plant a financial seed in, or you can donate to a charitable organization. If you don't have a job where you make money, you can certainly give of your time or talent. Tithing is about giving of your time, talent and possessions. If you have no possessions, then your time and your talent will both be sufficient in God's eyes according to scripture. I spoke earlier in the book about your talents and how we all have them, but it may take some searching to figure out what your specific talent is.

Once you have set aside your ten percent after you have been paid, it's now time to think about how much of your paycheck you want to save. Perhaps you can determine what you will save by determining what you are saving for. You may or may not have a specific purchase in mind and therefore nothing that really requires a strict savings plan. If you already have something in mind you are saving for, then you can figure out based on when you want to actually make the purchase, how much you will need to put away on a regular basis to achieve that financial goal.

Goal, there's that word again. Setting financial goals follows the same process discussed earlier in the section on goal setting, there's no difference when it comes to setting goals for your money usage. You have a target in mind, you figure out what you need to do to get there, including how much money will be needed, and how many hours you need to work, etc. You will need to go through the same process for setting financial goals as you would life goals.

Many teenagers and young adults often plan to purchase their first car. If you are blessed to have parents to purchase your first car for you, then this will not have to be a goal for you. But I am certain that there are other things you may have in mind to purchase that may require planning and goal setting.

In either case, setting a budget is necessary. Once you have determined what you are saving for, the planning can begin. Start by sitting down and figuring out what your expenses are for the week or month. That means, add up or track what you are spending your money on. Then add in other things that you may spend your money on, but not as often and may have inadvertently left out, also include what you plan to save each week or month to the total. Then ask yourself, "Are these all things I really need, can I live without any of these things, where can I cut back, and what can I reduce in order to save for my big purchase?" Keep in mind, once you have added these sums up, place that total against what you make on your job (take home pay), and see if you can actually afford to live the way you do. Why is this important? I'll get there in a minute.

Here's an example of what I am talking about:

I take home $500 a month working at a retail store while going to school. (Let's say I actually make $560 before taxes for the sake of easy calculations.)

Tithes $56/month

Shopping with friends $100/month

Dinner and movies with friends $75/month

Personal care items $20/month

Hair and nail care $75/month

Help Mom with a bill $25/month

Savings for car/college books $100/month

Total . . . . $451/month expenses
(That leaves me with an extra $49/month)

Okay, so this looks good on paper and is very realistic. There are several questions I'd like you to ponder about this scenario. If this were your situation, what would you do with the extra 49 dollars? If I am saving for a car and/or college, am I saving enough? Are there areas above where I can cut back and put more towards my savings?

You must be a critical thinker when it comes to your finances. Leave no stone unturned if you want to maximize your financial potential. The scenario above looks good and would be typical for someone your age. It could also look a little different for someone your age in that the amount you are spending each month could be more than the amount you bring home. For example your monthly expenses could be $620, but you are only bringing home $500. In this case, you would have overspent your budget by $120. Not good! This is certainly not a practice to begin as you start to make money. You want to always spend less than you bring home. When you are spending more than you make, you are living above your means (financial ability) and you are setting yourself up for long-term financial hardship. Bad money practices can have so many long-term negative repercussions. My heartfelt advice is to learn early how to spend wisely, save aggressively, and be a good steward over your money.

Some of you may already be familiar with credit cards (not ATM cards). If you are not yet familiar with them or have never used them, get ready, because credit is the way this country operates. That doesn't mean you have to operate this way.

Credit is simply getting something now without having to pay for it now. Within a month's time, a bill will come for you to pay in full or partial payment on the thing(s) that you purchased on your credit card. This is essentially getting something on credit. Now, this is not a bad thing. What is bad, however, is when you get something on credit, or use your credit card and you do not have a job that pays you enough money to afford the things you purchased on your credit card. Most people feel that's the purpose of credit, to get things you cannot afford right now. While that is partially true, there is a huge misunderstanding, and that is, if you cannot afford to pay for it with what you make within a three month period or less, then you can't afford to get it. This would also be another example of living beyond your means. It should never take you one year to pay off a $200 jacket you purchased at the department store. If it does take you a year or more to pay off the jacket, once the credit card company has tacked on what is called interest (the amount they are charging you to be able to use their card and get things on credit), you end up paying significantly more than the $200 it was priced at. When you think of it that way, is that jacket worth $300.

Again, if you can pay the purchase off in 3 months or less, then using the card is fine. You have to make smart purchases and use your credit card wisely. Before you use your card, ask yourself, "Do I really need this, are all my other financial obligations in order and paid up so I can pay this off when it comes due, can I wait until it goes on sale, could I find it cheaper somewhere else, and what's the worse that can happen if I don't get this?" I encourage you to ask yourself these questions because if you answer them honestly, they can help you make wise decisions about your spending and possibly save you from future financial heartache. Many people get into bad financial trouble because of credit cards and overspending.

The reason I want to call it to your attention now is because very soon, once you graduate from high school and apply to college or trade school, credit card companies will begin to solicit you (seek you out). They will offer you credit cards with high amounts of available funds for you to just have a spending-fest and get all those things you couldn't get before or that your parents wouldn't buy for you. Being able to pull out that card and buy, buy, buy somehow feels liberating for the moment. But when that monthly bill (statement) comes and you have no money to pay the bill in full, this is the beginning of your financial bondage if you take the bait. So what if you pay what is called the minimum due amount? While that shows good faith on your part, and let's the creditor know you are honoring your agreement to make payments, it still keeps you tied to them through the monthly interest they tack on to any amount that is not paid in full. And remember, you end up paying more for an item than what it would have cost you if you had paid cash and been done with it.

Credit cards will come at you from all different directions, believe me when I tell you this, and you will be so tempted to get one from whatever bank or department store will give you one. Not a good idea.

Having *one* credit card is good enough for you to start out with, if you must have one. I only say this because these days there is very little anyone can do without having a credit card. I don't, however, encourage you to ever get a department store credit card, the interest rates are too high and department store cards are unnecessary because you can use a major credit card (Visa, Discover, Master Card, American Express) for almost any purchases you want to make, including gas and groceries. The other reason I recommend allowing yourself *one* card, is because it is important for you to start building your credit because eventually you will want to make purchases like a car or home and having already established a good credit/payment history makes you look like a good candidate to lend money to in the eyes of the bank. Having more than one credit card at this time can be too much for you to manage and could possibly set you up for financial trouble.

Keep in mind your credit belongs to you. When banks decide to lend you money, they base it on your credit alone. For example, if you go ask your parents to loan you $100, they will loan it to you based on how well you have paid them back in the past, or how many other debts you have outstanding that may make it difficult for them to get their money back from you. They will only be looking at you and your ability to pay them back. So, if they loaned you money, and you turned around and loaned it to a friend of yours who didn't pay you back which resulted in you not being able to pay your parents back, then that is your fault. Your parents will be looking at you for the money because they gave it to you, not your friend. That is the same way banks look at your credit standing. So what I advise is for you to always protect your credit. Don't allow others to use your credit cards with the promise of paying you back before the bill comes due. He or she may have good intentions to pay you, but things happen and they may not be able to come up with the money. Unfortunately for you, the credit card company doesn't care that your friend could not give you the money to pay your bill, but they will still expect the bill to be paid on time, by you!

Just like you should hold your social security number close to your heart, so should you hold your credit card information close to your heart, and that includes debit cards too. Allowing others access to this can have long term repercussions if it's not used wisely. This means family members as well as friends. I don't believe anyone would intentionally set out to harm your financial credit standing, but it can happen and all they can do is apologize to you for what they have done, but you are left with the clean-up and that can be costly and could take years depending on what has been charged and subsequently not paid.

Be discreet about having a credit card. Once your friends learn you have one, they may expect you to use it for them with the promise to pay you back. They may even become offended or upset if you say no, because they may not understand the seriousness of protecting your individual credit. So the less number of people you let know you have it the better. Also, it may be especially difficult to say no to a family member, but set limits with them that you know you can cover even if they don't pay you. You may not be in a position to cover a lot if you are only working a part-time job, but at least they'll understand that you take this very seriously.

The most important thing I want to communicate to you here is, be wise when it comes to money, credit and spending.

In the scenario mentioned earlier with the $49 dollars left over, do you spend it or save it? Don't spend it if you don't have anything you really need to spend it on. Don't spend it just because you have it to spend. When you have an excess of cash, it's ok to put it into your savings until you have something you really need to use it for.

The reason why understanding how to save, spend, invest and budget are all very important is because at some point sooner than later you will no longer be the responsibility of your parents and you will be living on your own. While this may seem far off for some of you reading this book, others of you may be knocking on the door of your own place or may have already moved out of your parents' home and into your own.

You have to think about saving for your future, your immediate future and long-term future. You have been able to depend on your parents, but once you leave the nest of safety, who will you depend on then? You can not and should not depend on anyone but yourself to make sure your needs are met.

You can not and should not depend on your boyfriend to take care of you. I don't care if he's made you a lot of promises about what he will do for you and how he will take care of you. Things happen and he may not always be around. You should not depend on your friends to take care of you. Again, things happen that may be out of their control. You never want to put yourself in a position where you are left without a safety net because you thought someone else was holding it. You are likely to fall flat on your face or your back depending on which way you are facing when you fall.

Here's an idea, start setting financial goals for yourself. Think about a few things you'd like to have one day, and use the goal setting plan to help you reach those financial goals. I am certain you can do it! Spend some time reading about how to invest your money. It's pretty amazing to see your money grow with just a little effort. Imagine what putting a lot of effort into investing wisely would yield you. Be mindful of how you are spending your money, and determine if the purchases you are making are valuable or are you just throwing your money away. Always remember to be grateful for the financial blessings of God (they all come from him), give him what he requires and watch the continued blessings flow your way. Also, remember, if you don't show that you can handle your money wisely, it may be a while before you will get to the next level. God sees how we use our blessings and continues to bless us accordingly.

If you look ahead to your financial future and start planning today, even at a young age, you will be so much further ahead of the game than others who wait until they are already in their mid-twenties or older. This is important because it is the building block of your future in terms of financial security, being able to do the things you want without having to worry about where the money is going to come from. Start toward financial independence now by establishing your career path, setting your personal and financial goals; reward yourself later.

Notes

Chapter 18:
What is
Responsibility?

What does it mean to be responsible? Being responsible means answering for your own behavior, whatever that behavior may be. Standing to accept your role in any given situation is being responsible.

In many situations, you may not want to take responsibility for your actions even when you are the responsible party in a given situation. But as you grow and mature, it should become easier to take responsibility for your actions. It should become easier because you realize that the consequences of your actions belong to you and only you, in most cases.

Being responsible for something does not always have to yield negative consequences. Of course if you are responsible for taking your parents car without permission, and you get caught, well that's likely to get you in a world of trouble that could end with several negative consequences. You may end up losing telephone privileges, unable to go out friends for a few weeks, or even lose your driving privileges.

Being responsible can have positive results that can help you through your developmental process. What do I mean by that? As you grow and develop into a young woman and on into young adulthood, your responsibilities will grow as well.

While your parents take care of you until you become an adult (and for some even long after that), it is important that you, at this age, start to take responsibility for yourself and the things that directly involve and relate to you.

As a young woman, you need to be asking yourself, "What am I responsible for?" You are responsible for your body, your health, your finances (money), your decisions, your education, your job and your interactions with others.

I will take some time here to discuss in detail each of the things I have mentioned above and explain why they are your responsibility and how you should handle each of them.

Your Body/Your Health

Your body is God's temple. As I discussed earlier in the book, God will not dwell in an unclean place. It is your responsibility to take care of your body both inside and out.

By this time in school you should have already taken a class on health and should be aware of the many diseases and/or physical conditions that your body can be subjected to just by being unclean. Keeping yourself clean is not only a must for your own health, but for the health of others you come into contact with. Germs are an inevitable fact of life as well as a natural part of living. They are easily transferred because of the close nature we live in with others; but we don't need to help them along by being unclean.

Some of you reading this may be thinking: *Why is she talking about this? I already know this stuff.* You'd be surprised at how many people, especially young women, who don't give it a second thought and go on daily with unclean hands, mouths, teeth, and bodies.

You don't want to expose yourself to harsh chemicals, nor make yourself susceptible to germs and diseases which could be prevented by just being clean. You may have heard the saying, "Cleanliness is next to Godliness," well it's true if you think about it. If God will not dwell in an unclean place, and you are not clean, then you are not close to him. If he dwells in a clean temple, and you are clean, then cleanliness is next to Godliness. It makes sense to me.

Health

Taking care of your body means you are being health conscious and making decisions that are in the best interest for your body. It is important to know and understand your own body. Everyone's body is different and what your friends may be experiencing with their bodies may not necessarily be happening with your body.

There are certain important things that you should always be concerned about when it comes to your body.

Good Hygiene

Making sure that you bathe daily is very important for many reasons. Bacteria can live on your body and can cause infections in certain areas if not cleaned.

Bathing daily keeps you from carrying unwanted odors that could cause people to avoid you.

It is okay to carry deodorant, feminine spray and/or body powder in your purse, keep it in your locker, or backpack when allowed.

Try to make it a habit to freshen up during the day, especially if you participate in rigorous activities like sports or P.E. At times you may have an extra long day and won't be able to return home to shower. Take this opportunity to *freshen up* by using the above mentioned items that you are going to be carrying along with you.

Always make sure that you are flossing and brushing your teeth daily. Not brushing and flossing daily can cause numerous dental problems. These dental problems can include cavities, gum disease and halitosis (bad breath).

Making and Keeping your Doctor's Appointments

As young women, taking an active role in your health also means getting involved with making and keeping your own doctor's appointments.

Remember your appointment and make sure you are prepared when you visit the doctor.

Establishing a good relationship with your pediatrician/family doctor is very important. You want to choose a doctor you feel comfortable enough with to ask any questions you are concerned or just curious about concerning your body.

Before your visit, you should write down all your questions; and don't be shy about asking them.

Be honest with your doctor/nurse when they ask you questions. They are gathering this information to make sure they are doing everything they can to help you maintain your health. Even if you are embarrassed about your body or with what's going on with your body, don't hold anything back. Your doctor can only help you if you let him/her. He/she can only help you based on the information you give them, so be upfront and honest about your activities, behaviors and concerns.

If you are having any other problems like crying all the time, feeling sad, feeling afraid of people, feeling stressed out with family/school, or feeling tired all the time, please make sure you discuss these symptoms with your doctor. Taking care of your mental health is just as important as taking care of your physical health.

Exercise
Making exercise a part of your daily or weekly activities is very important. Getting into the habit of regularly exercising helps keep you in shape, helps burn calories and gives you more energy.

Taking a walk daily, running, doing aerobics, swimming, dancing, riding your bike, or just about any active movement are all good ways to stay active. If you choose to engage in an activity that you really enjoy, it will not feel like exercise at all.

Sitting on the sofa or in a chair all day long without any exercise is not good for your muscles. Healthy, toned muscles require movement. You have probably read about the alarming statistics on childhood obesity. While overeating is the underlying cause of childhood obesity, not enough exercise contributes to that obesity. Being sedentary adds to any obesity problem.

If you incorporate exercise into your daily routine, you will feel much better about your overall health.

Eating Healthy
All food is not created equally! By this I mean there are some foods that are healthy and good for you while others are not.

First of all, eat until you are full. However, once your stomach tells you that you are full, listen to it. If you don't learn to listen to it, you will have a tendency to overeat.

The types of foods you choose to eat will have a huge impact on your overall health, including weight.

Thin is not in! Starving yourself is not the answer to losing weight or maintaining your current weight. Making good food choices and engaging in regular exercise is the best way to stay healthy. Some people are naturally thin and are very healthy. If you are not naturally thin, that's ok. The important thing is to eat healthy, stay fit and learn to appreciate your body.

Make sure you are getting the proper servings each day of fruits, grains, meat/dairy, sugars and fats. For different age groups the servings are different. Remember, anything in excess is not good for you. Eating too much of anything on a regular basis (overeating) sets the stage for health problems later in life.

You may have heard people say that breakfast is brain food. Well it sure helps get you going for the day. Eating breakfast is very important. It doesn't have to be a big meal, but you should have something in the morning to get your day started. Breakfast helps to boost your energy level; otherwise you may become tired before midday rolls around.

It's not a crime to have potato chips, cookies, cake, pizza, chocolate, hamburgers, French fries as well as other foods high in sugar and fat, but it's a good idea to always eat those high fat snacks in moderation. From time to time having a salad with your hamburger instead of French fries or drinking bottled water instead of soda are both good substitutes. Choosing a fruit cup or a piece of fruit instead of cookies or chips is also a good choice. Eating lots of sugar-filled deserts and starchy foods doesn't give you energy as you may think, they actually slow you down.

Always drink plenty of water, especially when it's hot outside and/or you are participating in rigorous activities. Choose water over soft drinks and sugary fruit drinks. Water is always the better choice for you. Remember sugar will actually slow you down. It provides you with a very temporary boost only to cause your energy level to crash later on.

Learn to develop healthy eating habits if you are not already doing so. Doing this will help you live a long healthy life. It may not seem important to you now, but what you do today, the choices you make today will affect you for the rest of your life in one way or another. So make good choices about your health.

Sleep

The recommended amount of sleep per night for teenagers is 9.5 hours. Statistics report that most are only getting about 7.5 hours. Getting a good night's sleep each night is important. Why?

- Having the proper amount of sleep allows you to be more alert the next day. If you are a teenager and driving to school, being sleep deprived can result in an accident.

- Having the proper amount of sleep decreases moodiness.

- Having the proper amount of sleep decreases your risk of depression.

- Having the proper amount of sleep allows you to function at your highest and best level.

Remember, your body is God's temple, and your body is where he dwells. He wants you to take care of yourself inside and out, physically and spiritually. Do you want God to dwell in an unhealthy, unclean, broken-down temple as a result of you not taking care of yourself?

On Spiritual Health

It is not enough for us to just be physically healthy we must also be spiritually healthy. This means we must allow ourselves to be lead by the Spirit of God and do those things that we know are right and pleasing in God's sight. We can only do this if we are studying God's word and understand what is required of us a Christians.

2 Timothy 2:15 tells us to: ***Study to show thyself approved unto God, a workman that needeth not to be ashamed, rightly dividing the word of truth*** (KJV).

If you are studying the word of God and meditating on scripture, then it should be very clear as to what you need to do in your life. There are no gray areas when it comes to God's word. Everything is laid out in black and white. There may be scripture passages that you find difficult to understand or interpret because of the way they are written, but asking your pastor or a Sunday school teacher to help you may give you some clarity. You should also pray and ask God for understanding when you are having trouble understanding what his word is saying.

Proverbs 3:5-6 says: ***Trust in the Lord with all your heart and lean not to your own understanding. In all thy ways acknowledge him and he will direct your paths*** (KJV).

Verse 6 of Proverbs 3 makes it very clear that God is in control, and he will direct your paths—all of them. Your role is to let him guide you.

A good practice to establish is to set time aside for daily Bible reading, prayer and meditation. In the morning before school is a good time to set aside. I recommend morning because taking some time in the morning gets you off to a good start each day. Having this time in the morning clears your mind for the day so you are better able to focus and face the challenges of the day with scripture in your mind and on your heart.

Occasionally, you may not be able to have this time in the mornings, that doesn't mean you should not spend time with God at all. It just means that you should find a time of day that is a better option for your meeting with God. I recommend that you practice setting aside some devotional time daily regardless of what that time of day may be. The more you pray and study the word of God, the clearer his will for your life will become to you.

If you are unsure of how to get started with a daily Bible reading routine, let me offer a few suggestions.

- Get a subscription to a Christian magazine or one that offers daily scripture readings (i.e. Daily Word or Daily Bread).
- Check the back of your personal Bible for daily Bible readings.
- Go online to biblegateway.com for suggested readings.
- Utilize your Sunday school book as a guide to find daily reading suggestions.
- Each day, just open your Bible and wherever you land begin reading there for the day.
- Ask your pastor or Sunday school teacher for daily reading suggestions.

Prayer should be daily as well. Prayers don't have to be long, fancy or full of big words. God wants more than anything to hear from someone with a sincere and humble spirit. When you begin to pray, just speak from your heart and be sincere in whatever you are seeking, asking or praising God for in your life.

Sometimes my prayers don't include asking for anything. I just kneel down and begin to thank God for things in my life that I know would not be possible if he was not in control of my life. I praise him for things I take for granted on a daily basis that you wouldn't ordinarily think of as a blessing such as walking, talking, feeding myself, thinking clear sane thoughts, blinking my eyes, swallowing, breathing without a monitor—anything and everything I am thankful for at that moment.

If we actually thought about all the blessings of God just in our own lives, we couldn't thank him enough.

I can't stress the importance of going to Sunday school. Think of Sunday school the same way as you do your regular school. It is an avenue by which we learn the will and the way of God. We learn through examples laid before us throughout the Bible. Our Sunday school teachers are chosen to lead because they have an understanding of God's word just as your regular school teachers have over the subjects they teach.

Being a part of Sunday school allows you to learn with your peers and study together the word of God. It also allows you to be in fellowship with your peers in an environment that is Christ-centered and Bible-based. This is not to say that you can not study the word of God by yourself, but having others around who have read the lesson just like you, can help you come to a better understanding of what you have read. In addition, attending Sunday school provides you with opportunities to help your peers with their own life's journey.

Sunday school is obviously different from worship service. It is a learning environment that allows for dialogue and question and answer while worship service does not. Even though worship service includes a sermon that often brings some teaching with it, it is for the most part, time spent worshiping God through song and praise.

A note on prayer

It is always important to find quiet time for prayer and scripture reading. Our days are filled with so much information, some good stuff and some not so good stuff. We are often confronted with having to make decisions about things we are unsure of. We meet people who have our best interest at heart and some who don't. We watch television, listen to music and read other media that is not always good for our spirit. So at the end of the day we may need to take time to cleanse our souls of the unclean things we have encountered throughout the day and ask God to not allow these things to dwell in us.

You've probably heard the phrase "garbage in/garbage out." If you constantly allow into your spirit negativity, that is what you are likely to display to others. Always be mindful of what effect a person or media tool is having on your spirit when you are reading, watching television or having a conversation with someone who has a foul mouth or is speaking things that are untrue.

Your Body Is a Temple

Do you not know that your body is a temple of the Holy Spirit, who is in you, whom you have received from God, you are not your own (1 Cor 6:19, NIV).

Drugs & Alcohol

Drugs and alcohol are poisonous to our bodies. There are many types of drugs out there that can have various effects on our bodies. While people may tell you that using drugs and alcohol will make you feel good, help you deal with your pain or make you feel grown up, what they aren't telling you, is that these substances can kill you. Or you can even become addicted— which is sometimes worse than death.

More importantly than just the consequences of introducing drugs or alcohol to our bodies is the fact that our bodies are God's temple. If we are putting poisonous substances into our bodies, then we are abusing God's temple.

There are certain things I'd like to point out to you about drugs and alcohol that I believe you must understand before contemplating the use of these substances and how they can affect you and your body.

1. Developing a tolerance for alcohol is not a good thing because over time you must use more of that particular substance to obtain the high you received during your first use. The more you use, the more dangerous it becomes for you to use. You can die from just one instance of drug overdose or alcohol poisoning. So when someone says, "I have a high tolerance for alcohol" or "I can hold a lot of alcohol," please don't see this as a good thing. It's not a good thing at all.

2. Using drugs/alcohol reduces your ability to make wise, sound decisions. If you are under the influence of drugs or alcohol, you may fall into a trap where someone can take advantage of you sexually— rape or molest you. Someone may even take your inebriated state as an opportunity to rob you or steal from you without you being aware of what is going on until it is too late.

3. Being under the influence hampers your reflexes and reduces your ability to respond quickly and effectively. If you are driving a car, you could have an accident that could injure or kill yourself or someone else. (You might hear some people say that they feel they do their best work when they are high, or they drive better when they are under the influence. This is all in their head and perhaps they have never been tested to think on their feet while in this state. Don't believe them; listen to the statistics and research that is provided to you in your schools and by your parents.)

The use of drugs and/or alcohol can ruin your life. If you think *trying it out* is all you want to do, Think Again! *Trying it out* can be the one time you use and all it takes to get you hooked. You have seen people on the streets or in movies and may have even laughed at them because they were drunk or *cracked out*, It might be funny to see, but it wouldn't be funny if it were you that everyone was laughing and talking about. You don't need to even try these substances if you are acknowledging your body as God's temple and not your own.

If you are currently using drugs or alcohol, STOP NOW! If you believe that because you have been using and you haven't gotten hooked you're safe, don't be so certain, addiction doesn't look the same for everyone. The more you use, the more you are increasing your chances of becoming addicted. If you have been using, and you're concerned about your usage, please talk with your parents, a teacher or school counselor to get help immediately.

Marijuana and alcohol are what are considered *gateway drugs*. This means if you begin using these drugs even a little bit to begin with, you are more likely to open yourself up to using other drugs that may be stronger and harder in the future. These two drugs create a gateway from no use at all to using heavier drugs.

Using drugs and alcohol takes a tremendous toll on your temple. While you may not be able to see it in the early years of your life (teenage years), over time using can cause physical problems, medical problems, mental problems and various skin problems. Some of those problems include:

- Sclerosis of the liver
- Paranoia
- Dry mouth & throat
- Sleepiness
- Increased heart rate
- Impaired short-term memory

Many people use drugs and alcohol to help them cope with life's problems. If you are having problems such as relationship issues, family problems, stressing about grades, or whatever you may be having trouble with, talk to someone you trust about these problems. Please don't try to work them out alone or use drugs to help you deal with the challenge. Using will only make you feel better for the moment. Your problems will still be there when you come down for your high, and you run the risk of long term addiction.

Learning how to effectively deal with your problems will take you a long way in life. It is better to confront problems head on rather than to put them off or self medicate with drugs or alcohol. Your problems will never go away—they will get worse.

Try to always remember your body is God's temple. What you do to your body, you are doing to God. *Really!*

Your Money

In the last chapter I discussed the importance of financial planning which included saving money and spending it wisely. I also talked about setting financial goals that will help you get in position to financially care for yourself. The emphasis for this section is to help you understand how important your money is to you.

You are solely responsible for the money you make. This means no one else can actually make your money for you. If *you* go to work, then *you* get paid. If you choose to work 20 hours in one week, then you will get paid for working those 20 hours for that week. No one else can work your job for you, and you will still be the person that ends up getting a paycheck, unless you own the business. For the sake of this discussion, let's assume you are working for someone, and they are paying you. The hours you work will be the hours you are paid for. Where am I going with this? Just as you work and earn your own money, you should spend your own money.

I am not suggesting that you become selfish and not have a heart to share or bless others with what you have, but blessing someone is different than taking care of someone. Many times young women get in the habit of *taking care* of their boyfriends. You are not in a position to take care of anyone, especially if you are working only part-time. Even if you are working fulltime, your focus is to take care of your own responsibilities first. Besides, if you are working part-time, then that means someone, probably your parent(s), is still taking care of you. What would it look like for you to become someone else's sponsor when you have one of your own, your parents?

In talking about being responsible with your money, you must make wise decisions about how you spend your hard-earned money and on whom you spend it. Sure, you may want to buy your boyfriend or friends gifts for birthdays or other special occasions, and that is ok to do. What I am suggesting is that you think of yourself. If you find yourself spending more on others with little left for yourself to reach the goals you have set, then you should probably rethink your spending and focus more on your savings.

I am not saying you shouldn't buy for others, but be reasonable and ask yourself why are you buying this item for this person? As a matter of fact, I think a person who has a heart of giving is quite unselfish. However, don't allow your giving heart to been seen as a weakness that could get you taken for a ride.

The money you make is to take care of you. You earn money to help your parents out in areas such as your entertainment, your extra curricular activities, dining with friends and other personal care necessities, as well as to contribute to some savings for your future. While getting a job may not be a requirement of your parents, if you choose to get one, start thinking about how you can be responsible for the things you desire for yourself. Learn how to be responsible for caring for your personal needs. Mom or Dad won't always be around or willing to take care of your financial needs forever.

Remember, no one can spend your money but you, so when it's all spent you are the one to look to for how responsible you have been in your spending. You're responsible for how it gets spent, so do you want to spend it wisely, or frivolously? It's your call, so be responsible!

Your decisions

Yes that's right. You *are* responsible for the decisions you make. Bad decisions will come back to haunt you, good ones will make you proud.

Of course in this life we will make some decisions that are bad, or at best decisions that result in some not-so good-consequences. Making a couple of bad decisions doesn't mean it's the end of the world. Actually, if you are fortunate, you can occasionally turn bad decisions into valuable lessons learned. The saying, "Experience is the best teacher" is true. Well that can be the case with making a bad decision. Through that experience, you learn not to do that again. The thing to be clear about regardless of what you decide is that it is your decision; consequently the outcome is your responsibility. You may have also heard the saying, "If you make your bed, you have to lay in it." Again the decisions you make are yours and yours alone, and you will be held accountable for any and all of the ones you make.

So why do I offer these observations? I offer them because I want you to make good decisions that will yield good results. You may not always make the best decision in every situation, but let's agree that you will learn from all your decisions. Below please keep in mind a few things I think you can do to keep from making poor decisions.

- Take each situation and look at the decisions that need to be made in that situation as separate from any decisions you've ever made before. Even though a situation may resemble something you have had to deal with before, it's probably not the same thing. So begin your evaluation process as though it's new. Of course you always want to draw from previous experiences, especially those that turned out in your favor, but beginning with a clean slate will help you sort through all the facts and leave no stone unturned.

- Give each situation due diligence. Don't make quick decisions about things that truly require some thought and time. There will be times when you will have to make a split-second decision or respond more quickly than usual. Quick decisions will not always be the case, and you should not make it a practice of making a quick decision. Instead, allow yourself time to think things through and come up with the best possible solution for you.

- Pray about the situation. We should never go it alone, so prayer can help you get to where you need to be in any situation. If you don't receive an answer, then maybe you should just be still until you get one, through prayer. It is important to understand that waiting may feel impossible and unbearable, but trying to correct a mistake made in haste can be even more frustrating.

- Try not to agree to anything right away. People will ask you to do things for them or with them, and sometimes you may agree without thinking about it and end up regretting your decision later. An agreement doesn't have to be something bad that you have agreed to, but it may be something that you really don't want to do now. It may just be an agreement that if you actually thought about would be something that you can't afford to do financially or is a time-consuming commitment that you don't have time to fulfill, and now you are stuck because you have already committed. If someone asks you to do something, make it a practice to let them know you will think about it and get back with them on it.

Taking time to think about a matter keeps you from having to squirm out of something, or go at something halfheartedly. An example of this would be, someone asking you to be the new president of the teen club at your church. You agree to do it without giving it some thought, and then you find yourself unable to fulfill the commitment because you have school, choir, track, and band to contend with. You may continue on as president, but you are not giving it your all, and a big part of you wishes you had not agreed to accept the position to begin with.

- Ask yourself, how is this going to affect me? When asking yourself this question, think about the long-term effects of the decision. Will it add value to my life? Will I be ashamed of myself? Will my parents be proud to hear of this decision? Will others be hurt as a result of my doing this? Will I regret this decision in the morning or the next day? What could I lose or gain from this decision? Is it worth my time and energy? All these questions should be answered before making a decision. I'm sure you can probably think of a few more that could help you along in making good choices.

- Be sure of the choice you've made. If you are not sure about the decision you've made, then it may not be the right one for you. Sometimes we know beyond a shadow of a doubt that what we have decided is the right thing. Other times we are unsure or a little less certain. It's in those uncertain times that you must reevaluate your decision to do something before you've actually done it and think it through once more.

- Weigh out the decision. Create a pros and cons list to help you determine if you should move forward with a particular choice or not.

- Do a cost benefit analysis. What is that? Almost along the lines of the item above, a cost benefit analysis means you take a situation in which you must make a decision about, and you weigh the total expected cost (time, money, effort, etc.) against the total expected benefit.

We all will make good decisions and bad ones, but they are ours to make nonetheless, and no one else will be responsible for them, so make sure you keep that in mind. Following the above suggestions could, in some cases, save you a lifetime of pain and unnecessary heartache, oh and a few do-overs too.

Your education

In most states you can stop attending school after you reach a certain age if you want. While I would not advise anyone to do this, it is certainly your call to make and therefore your responsibility to deal with the consequences of such a drastic decision.

Why would I discourage dropping out of school or not attending college or trade school beyond high school? Well first of all, it's absurd to think that you would have received all the knowledge you need to further yourself in this world and make a decent living for yourself by the age of 16, 17 or 18. While you may have acquired a lot of street smarts, that doesn't get you far in the real world of survival. Furthermore, after you have finished playing around and decide to get serious about your life, you will then realize that you made a huge mistake (one that could be costly) and begin to regret choosing to leave school early or having stopped furthering your education.

I say it is a huge and costly mistake because you can neither turn back the hands of time nor make up for lost time. What you have lost here is time, and to begin correcting the problem could cost you a lot of money that could have otherwise been spent on something to propel yourself forward.

If you are one of the many teenagers who has dropped out of school or decided not to further your education beyond high school, it doesn't have to be the end of the road for you. You are allowed to change your mind. Remember, *your* decisions are *your* responsibility as is your education. I would hope that you would create in yourself a desire to do something different. I would hope that sooner rather than later you see that having made a decision to drop out was not one that has had the best possible outcome for your life and be encouraged to make the decision to return to an institution of higher learning.

While you are still in school, some important things to keep in mind is to focus on your grades, be serious about making good grades and maintain a higher than average GPA. A lot of people think they have all the time in the world to make good grades or turn their GPA around. This is typically not true and that kind of thinking can set you up for a huge disappointment. Before you know it, your senior year will be upon you, and you'll want to go to college. If you have not been making good grades you may find it hard to get into the college you want or even graduate on time. Take you grades seriously early on in your school career. Start your freshman year with the attitude that good grades are necessary even if they don't come easy. Working hard in the beginning makes the final stretch less stressful. If you buckle down and stay focused in the early years of high school, then when you get to your senior year, you won't find yourself trying to make up for lost time.

A lot of people take the attitude that only their junior- and senior-year grades matter. While these two years are important, your GPA matters more. And your GPA is based on all course work done in high school, including freshman and sophomore years. So if you do well the last two years of school but make average or less than average grades the first two years that affects your overall GPA which is what colleges look at when evaluating your application.

This is also the case with college. Begin your college career with an attitude of determination to succeed. That means start out on the right foot, make good grades and get a tutor in a difficult class early on, if need be. Don't wait until mid-semester when half of your grades are already earned to decide you need help. I guarantee that the more work you put in on the front end of your college career, the easier you will breathe on the back end.

Don't wait until your last year of high school or college to start trying to turn things around. You will be stressed out and probably disappointed when you learn that you are either not going to graduate on time or not at all. Getting a good education is worth the work and putting certain things on hold until you get it is certainly worth the sacrifice.

Having an education is vitally important. A good education is your ticket to long-term job success. There use to be a time when a high school diploma was all you needed. Then there was a time when a college degree (a bachelor's degree from a 4-year college) was a great thing. Now it seems as though you must continue on to get a master's degree or even a Ph.D. in order to be competitive in the job market. Of course depending on the field of work you plan to go into, none of these may be required, but be mindful of the fact that higher education is a must or it may be hard for you to get very far. You can't just stop after high school.

As I mentioned before, college is not for everyone, but everyone will eventually have to take care of themselves one day. Wouldn't you want to be able to take care of yourself in the best possible way? Afford yourself the opportunity to learn a skill or trade that you can market, get a college degree that can put you in a top paying job along with your peers, and develop skills that can set you apart from others. Whatever you do, make sure you are taking responsibility for your education because it is the one thing that will take you to the next level in your career or job.

Your job

Your job is your responsibility. Your employment is what will help sustain the lifestyle you create for yourself one day. So make sure that whatever you decide to do for a living is satisfactory to you and is something you can see yourself doing for a long time.

Of course, over time you can expect to change jobs several times. You may even change careers. Keep in mind, it is your responsibility to choose a field that you are excited about, feel comfortable working in, and can see yourself growing in. There's nothing worse career-wise than to get into a situation that you didn't create for yourself and have to live with the regret of doing something you don't want to do. Many people fail to take responsibility for decisions about their jobs/careers and wind up very unhappy or unsatisfied with the work they end up doing. But at the end of the day, it's still their responsibility and their decision.

If you are blessed with a job, whether you love it or not, make sure you give it one hundred percent. It doesn't matter if you are working at McDonald's, Macy's or VH1 as a summer intern, show your employer that you are a great employee and you have ambition and drive. This is part of the responsibility you must take on in order to get you to the next level in your career. All the experiences you are allowed to have while working will prepare you for the next job and then the next job. You should make it your business to learn something from all your work experiences.

Lessons are like building blocks. Stack them wisely one on top of the other, and you can create something wonderful. If you use the lessons you learn from each work experience, you can become a more desirable employee to have, you can be sharper and more astute in your decision making processes, and an overall better employee than you were before.

When you have been given opportunities by your employer to do things that may carry a little more responsibility, take advantage of those opportunities without feeling you have to get paid extra for it. I encourage you to ask for a raise if your job description all of a suddenly changes drastically from what you were hired to do; but if requests are made from time to time by your employer for you to do something out of the scope of your job that doesn't put you in harm's way or cause you to be grossly inconvenienced, then do it. Consider such a request an opportunity to learn more as well as an opportunity to build your resume with new skills.

Don't allow your friends or people you know (family included) to get you in trouble with your job. Don't get in the habit of taking things from your employer to give to your friends. If your employer allows you to eat free, that's for you, not for your friends or family. If your employer allows you to use a store discount, unless they tell you that your friends and family members can use it too, then it's for only you. Friends and family as well may try to get you to do favors for them through your employer. It may be difficult for you to say no to them, but remember your job is your responsibility, and if you get fired because you were helping out a friend, then you get fired on your own. No one made you do what you did, and therefore no one is responsible for that decision except you. Of course you would like to blame someone else when you goof, especially if you can justify your lapse in judgment because you "did it for them," but your employer has the right to hold only you accountable for your actions because you are the person who works for them.

Make it a point to read your employee handbook and make yourself aware of all the do's and don'ts of your company. This is your responsibility. Your employer will give you a copy of the rules, but unlikely to go over each and every one of them with you. Find out what is acceptable and what isn't when you are on the job. Ask questions about anything you are unclear about or doesn't make sense to you. Again, you will be held responsible for your part in knowing and following the rules as an employee.

Ultimately, you are responsible for your job, what you do with it, and how successful you are at it. Your efforts as a reliable employee can take you a long way or not. Never go into a job situation with the attitude that it's just a means to an end, or it's just something to get you by. While that may be the case, if you carry that attitude, the attitude will be obvious in how you do your work and the value you place on the company you work for. You never know, you may start out as a clerk when you are 16 years old, but end up being the store manager by the time you are 22 years old. However, you will only get to that managerial position if you have the right attitude and show your employer that you are willing to give your job a 100 percent effort regardless of the position you have or how long you plan to keep it.

Learning to be responsible and accepting responsibility for your actions is a sign of maturity. Understanding the things in your life for which you are responsible and being held accountable, places you in a position of distinct advantage over your peers. You do not want to go through life blaming others or expecting others to do what you are responsible for doing or what you can and should do for yourself. When you have a clear picture of what your place in this world looks like, making good choices will begin to come naturally for you.

Notes

Chapter 19:
One Final Note

You possess what it takes to be successful in life, you have to believe that about yourself and challenge yourself to be the best you can be.

How do you do that?

1. Believe in yourself.

2. Work hard in school.

3. Work diligently at your jobs.

4. Choose positive friends.

5. Choose positive role models and mentors.

6. Fill your mind with things of substance (the Bible, books or magazines on the world, finance, investing, and entrepreneurship) It's ok to listen to rap music, pop music, rock music and R&B, or to read romance novels once in a while, but how far are those things really going to take you in the world.

7. Venture outside of your comfort zone from time to time.

8. Go the extra mile; don't settle for doing just the minimum.

9. Walk with your shoulders up and back, not sagging downward. People see confidence when you hold your head up and shoulders back. They see insecurity and a lack of self confidence when your shoulders and head are down.

10. Tell yourself everyday that you have a purpose for being on this earth because you do. You just have to find your purpose.

11. Write out your dreams and avoid people who say you can't do or be something you want to do or be.

It's not okay for you to sit back and accept mediocrity. You must command respect for yourself. You must first respect yourself and others. Each generation is given more opportunities than the generations before, so you have no excuse to do nothing or be nothing. Many opportunities await you, but no one is going to chase you down to give an opportunity to you. You have to want it and go get it. God says, *"Ask and it shall be given to you* (Matt 7:7, NIV).

As I bring this book to a close, I hope you begin to understand where your place is in this world, what you must do to reach your highest and best level, and what God's purpose is for your life. Remember we all have special gifts and talents and must use them to glorify God in whatever way we can. Don't be afraid to shine in the areas you know God has truly blessed you. Don't allow others to tell you something contrary to what you know and believe to be good and true about you. A pertinent passage of scripture to keep in mind is, ***Every good and perfect gift is from above, coming down from the Father of the heavenly lights, who does not change like shifting shadows*** (James 1:17, NIV). Please remember you are a precious gift from God, and you are good and perfect. Anyone who says otherwise is wrong about you. You must always, always believe that!

I now challenge you to spend time with your girlfriends having quality, in-depth discussions about your life, your future, and how you can be the best you can be. Spend less time on idle chatter that adds little value to your life, and instead strive to grow in ways that you probably never thought possible.

Notes

Work Section
and Guide to a Better You

Your answers to the questions in this section of the book are not right or wrong. Don't rush through the questions and answer them all at once, take your time. Give each question serious thought and only put down your heartfelt answers. You don't have to feel obligated to share any of your answers with other people. However I encourage you to have an open discussion with your girlfriends about the things you've learned in this book.

Have fun going through this section of the book, and enjoy learning more about who you are and who you hope to become.

Chapter 1– Self Respect

1. What are some ways you have allowed people to disrespect you in the past?

2. What are some things you can do to gain respect or command respect?

3. Why is self respect important to you?

Chapter 2– Love Yourself

1. How can you show yourself love?

2. In what ways have you neglected to show love for yourself?

Chapter 3 – Set Standards for Yourself

1. What is your value system and what do you value most in your life?

2. What do you value most in your friendships?

3. What do you value most in other people?

4. What are some standards that you live by?

5. What does the way you dress communicate about you?

Chapter 4– Believe In Yourself

1. What am I most good at doing?

2. What have people close to me said I am most good at doing?

3. I am the happiest when I am _____.

4. What are the things that present the most challenge for me to accomplish my dreams?

Chapter 5 – Can Anyone Get Me to Do Something I Don't Want to Do?

1. Discuss a time when you felt you were under pressure to do something you didn't want to do.

2. Discuss how that made you feel.

Chapter 6 – Abusing Your Temple

1. Today I commit to stop _____ because I know that doing this is abusing my temple and it is not pleasing to God.

2. What do you need to forgive yourself for and ask God to forgive you for?

Chapter 7 – Beauty, Is It Really Only Skin Deep?

1. Does my attitude turn people away from me or draw people toward me?

2. How do you think other people see you?

3. How do you see yourself?

4. How do you want other people to see you?

5. If your friends were interviewed about you, what words would they most likely use to describe you?
   a. How would you feel about their description of you?

6. My description of a beautiful person is: _____
   _____.

Chapter 8 – Your Heritage

1. Where do I come from? What is my heritage (family ancestry, family name, state, etc.)?

2. What are some things that make me proud/sad about my heritage?

3. Who has impacted my life the most in my family? Why?

4. What do I want my legacy to be? How do I want to be remembered by my peers in high school, college, coworkers, friends and family?

5. Why do I want this to be my legacy?

Chapter 9 – Healthy Relationships

1. What are the most important elements in a relationship to you?

2. How do you define a healthy relationship?

3. Are you holding any grudges against anyone you feel has wronged you?

4. Is there anyone in your life you need to forgive?

5. How will know that you have really forgiven that person? What will that feel like for you?

6. Has anyone ever abused you in a relationship? How will you now work to get this person out of your life if you have not already done so?

7. How important is it for you to have a boyfriend at this point in your life? Why, or why not?

8. How long are you willing to wait for the right guy to come along? Why would you wait?

Chapter 10 – Communication and Relationships

1. What is the difference between communication and effective communication?

2. How can you make sure that what you are communicating is received the way you intended for it to be received?

3. In what ways can you become a better communicator than you already are?

Chapter 11 – To Whom Can You Turn When Your Relationship Is in Trouble?

1. How comfortable do you feel talking to your parent (s) about a negative situation in your relationship? Why do you feel this way?

2. Can you turn to both or either parent for help?

3. Is there anyone else besides your best friend that you could turn to?

Chapter 12 – Friendship

1. How important is friendship to you?

2. What are you willing to invest in your friendships?

3. Have you ever compromised your beliefs in order to be friends with someone?

4. What do you value most in your friendships?

5. Would you tell your friend the truth even if it hurt them? Why, or why not?

6. Would you want your friend to tell you the truth even if it hurt you? Why, or why not? What wouldn't you want to know the truth about?

Chapter 13— College/ Career

1. What is my plan after high school or college?

2. How committed are you to putting your best foot forward to bring that plan to fruition?

3. How will you determine the direction that is best for you vs. what someone else feels you should do?

Chapter 14 — Let's Talk about Goal Setting

1. Set some goals now.
    a. Where do you want to be in 5 years?

    b. Where do you want to be in 10 years?

2. What is it going to take for me to get there?

3. What kind of investment am I willing to make to get there?

4. What are some realistic things you want to accomplish?

Chapter 15 – Research

1. My current method used in researching has been _____.

2. What are other forms of research you can use?

3. Through research I have ruled out becoming a _____.

4. Through research I feel _____ and _____ are viable career options for me.

Chapter 16 – Habits of Excellence

1. Of the nine habits of excellence, which one(s) comes the easiest for you to do? Why?

2. Which one presents the most challenge for you? Why?

Chapter 17 – Financial Planning and Budgeting

1. What are some financial goals you have set for yourself?

2. How important to you is your credit standing?

3. What steps will you go through to protect your credit?

4. How will you begin to save money for your future?

5. Who are you depending on to support you after you leave home?

6. Create a budget for yourself based on the money you currently earn or receive from your parents for one month. Write out on a separate sheet of paper.

7. What resources will you use to learn more about spending, saving and investing?

8. Why would you invest in the stock market or real estate?

9. Have you ever been let down by someone you have loaned money to? How do you plan to keep from letting that happen again?

Chapter 18 – What Is Responsibility?

1. Who is ultimately responsible for the decisions you make?

2. What things can you do to better take care of your health?

3. What things are you currently doing that you would like to change about your health?

4. What process will you use to determine the best course of action for a particular situation in your life?

5. How can you continually make good health, diet and financial decisions for yourself?

6. If you were going to make a big change in your life after having read this book, what would that change(s) be? Why?

Acknowledgements and Special Thanks

God, thank You for placing in me the desire to want to be obedient to your word, your will and your way. You are truly an awesome God.

Cofi, Lauren and Caleb, thank you for giving me space to write. Your daily love, hugs and smiles renewed my drive to complete this necessary work.

Albert and Donnie McGee, who I have affectionately called Mommy and Daddy all my life, thanks for setting me up to be successful in whatever I chose to do by introducing me to God early in my life. Your words have always encouraged and never torn down anything I wanted to do. For that I thank you both.

Renee, Rosalyn, Joyce, LaTonya and Albert Jr., your continued love and support through the years have encouraged me beyond belief. I love and thank you all so much.

Dawn "Nicki" Patterson, you have been so supportive over the years, I love and thank you because I know you will always tell me truth and encourage me through the word of God.

Dena, thank you for being my biggest cheerleader, even in those times I didn't think I had anything to cheer about. You are a dear heart! I love you.

Claudette, I am so grateful to God for your strength, laughter, encouragement, and friendship over the years. You have cheered me on because you often saw something in me that I didn't always see. Thank you!

Nicole Smith and Panacea Publishing, thanks for believing in this project and working hard to help me make this happen. You have truly been a blessing!

Pastor Ware and Rev. JT Ware and the Mt. Olive Baptist Church, thanks for your love and for giving me a peaceful place to worship. I thank God for you all.

To all my Miss Pearl 2007 contestants, Akevan Symone, Nikigera, Fontashia, Jennifer, and Breanna, thanks for the ride, it was truly a labor of love, you all were great! My love for you all confirms why this book is so important to me.

To all my friends who have so richly blessed my life through your words of encouragement, support, friendship, laughter in times of sorrow, and just plain being there when I needed you, thank you so much. You all know who you are, God bless you!

To my nieces, Krista and Ebony, you both have inspired my efforts towards this project because you both are beautiful young women that I so much desire happiness and love for in your lives from all the right people and relationships.

To the rest of my family, I love you all so much, you have no idea. Thanks for having me!

Lastly, to all the women who I have had the opportunity to meet over the years, you have inspired my heart in so many ways, and if you are reading this book, just know that I write for you. Be blessed by the words of this book, and thank you for allowing me the pleasure of knowing you.

Notes

The following pages can be used for you to write down feelings, thoughts or questions you may have while reading this book. You may also use this section to complete assignments if you are using this book as part of a class or workshop.

Notes

Notes

Notes

About The Author

Andrea J. Adams established The Rapha Agency in 2003. She has a master's degree in Community Counseling from Columbus State University, and is a licensed professional counselor (LPC) in Georgia. She works with adolescents, couples, families and individuals in her private practice. She has also worked with clients and their families dealing with the effects of alcohol and drug addiction. She has many years working in the counseling field and believes that each and every person holds inside themselves the ability to effect change in their own lives. She feels her role as a counselor is to help them realize that ability. She is committed to helping young women become their best regardless of the obstacles they face. She is married with two children and resides in metro Atlanta.

Email Andrea at: adamsandrea76@yahoo.com
or visit **www.ifweweregirlfriends.com**

Made in the USA